RUTH PRETTY ENTERTAINS

Penguin Books

PENGUIN BOOKS
Published by the Penguin Group
Penguin Group (NZ), 67 Apollo Drive, Rosedale,
North Shore 0632, New Zealand (a division of Pearson New Zealand Ltd)
Penguin Group (USA) Inc., 375 Hudson Street,
New York, New York 10014, USA
Penguin Group (Canada), 90 Eglinton Avenue East, Suite 700, Toronto,
Ontario, M4P 2Y3, Canada (a division of Pearson Penguin Canada Inc.)
Penguin Books Ltd, 80 Strand, London, WC2R 0RL, England
Penguin Ireland, 25 St Stephen's Green,
Dublin 2, Ireland (a division of Penguin Books Ltd)
Penguin Group (Australia), 250 Camberwell Road, Camberwell,
Victoria 3124, Australia (a division of Pearson Australia Group Pty Ltd)
Penguin Books India Pvt Ltd, 11, Community ½½Centre,
Panchsheel Park, New Delhi – 110 017, India
Penguin Books (South Africa) (Pty) Ltd, 24 Sturdee Avenue,
Rosebank, Johannesburg 2196, South Africa

Penguin Books Ltd, Registered Offices: 80 Strand, London, WC2R 0RL, England

First published by Penguin Group (NZ), 2008
1 3 5 7 9 10 8 6 4 2

Copyright © text, Ruth Pretty, 2008
Copyright © photographs, Murray Lloyd, 2008

The right of Ruth Pretty and Murray Lloyd to be identified as the author and photographer of
this work in terms of section 96 of the Copyright Act 1994 is hereby asserted.

Designed and typeset by Seven.co.nz
Prepress by Image Centre Ltd
Printed by Everbest Printing Co. Ltd, China

ISBN 978 014 300980 1

A catalogue record for this book is available
from the National Library of New Zealand.

www.penguin.co.nz

RUTH PRETTY ENTERTAINS

Ruth Pretty

Photography by Murray Lloyd

Penguin Books

CONTENTS

Acknowledgements 6

Introduction 7

ONE Drinks 9

TWO Summer 33

THREE Winter 57

FOUR Posh 81

FIVE Celebrations 105

SIX Coffee 131

SEVEN Condiments 149

Index 172

Acknowledgements

A big thank you to everyone at Ruth Pretty Catering. You are all experts at juggling balls. In particular thanks to Jo Tracey, chef in charge of the Ruth Pretty Cooking School and of recipe development, who every day makes a difference in our kitchen but especially for her work towards this book. Thanks to Avril Grant, kitchen manager, for organising the production to happen every day. Thanks to Jess Christensen, chef, who worked with me to present the food for Murray Lloyd's photographs.

Thank you to Murray Lloyd. It is always a pleasure to work with Murray.

Thanks to Robyn Mitchell for compiling the manuscript and all the work you do every day on recipes. Thank you to Renny Brown for making the days run so smoothly.

Thank you to Dorothy Vinicombe and Catherine O'Loughlin, my publisher and editor at Penguin respectively. Thank you to the team at Seven for their design work.

Paul and I would like to dedicate this book to Ruth Pretty Catering and the spirit of so many parties past. Thank you to our customers, staff and suppliers for a great twenty years and we believe we have at least another twenty to create wonderful occasions for special people. A heartfelt dedication to our longest serving team member, Paul's mother Margaret McNaughton, who to this day does not miss a trick.

Introduction

As a little girl I always liked being in charge and stole the roles of mother, queen or bride in games. At the age of seven I was fired from Brownies because I couldn't be part of a team. I didn't mind my dismissal, as I am left–right blind and didn't want my subordinates to see I was having trouble with knots.

Neighbours gave me a large wooden appliance crate, which my father adjusted so it could be my playhouse, and this is where I began to entertain. I had tea sets, pots and an oven made from a carton. I would invite younger children in our street to eat my dandelion and mud stew seated at a fruit-crate table, which I took the time to lay before they arrived.

Throughout my childhood I hung out with Mum in the kitchen, helping to make the gravy, preparing vegetables and learning about baking so that by the time I was a teenager I could cook dinner.

My father has always said my two sisters and I thrive on the sound of applause. He unfortunately has always called this trait 'the clap-clap'. To nurture our desire for centre stage, our mother enrolled us in elocution classes, nowadays referred to as speech and drama classes. Spanning a period of 20 years, we individually visited Mrs Goodson once a week to recite poems, read passages from Dickens or portray characters such as the Red Queen from *Alice in Wonderland*. Elocution exams and May- and August-holiday competitions were part of our lives. My mother was a brilliant at sewing so we always had the best costumes. Mrs Goodson had high hopes for us and felt my younger sister, Christine, was her star pupil.

None of us made it to the stage professionally, but my elder sister, Anne, is a consummate storyteller, Christine at the drop of a hat will re-enact Liza Minnelli's entire role in the film *Cabaret,* including the songs, and I give cooking classes.

In one way or another, entertaining has always been at the forefront of my life.

This cookbook is all about terrific recipes so that when you entertain you will receive applause, and I hope this inspires you to relax and be yourself so you can entertain with personality.

ONE

DRINKS

There are many occasions when you want to entertain friends but you, or they, don't have much time. You need to fit them in around so many other activities. Your lack of time may mean there is no way you can prepare dinner for them, so drinks it is. In your house this form of entertaining may go by the name of 'drinkie-poos', 'wine-o-clock', 'elevenses' or 'fiveies'. You may describe it as 'when the sun is over the yardarm' or my favourite euphemism for a few drinks – 'two drinks and bugger off'. Whatever you call it, having friends around for wine or cocktails, perhaps even coffee or tea, interesting non-alcoholic drinks and incredibly moreish easy-to-eat food is relaxing for everyone.

Dave's Prosciutto Rolls

Makes 15–18 serves

120 g (6) paper-thin slices prosciutto

20 g (2 tbsp) Sandwich Mayonnaise (see page 152)

25 g (3 handfuls) rocket leaves

35 g shaved Parmesan

60 g (4) dried figs (thinly sliced)

30 ml (2 tbsp) balsamic syrup

freshly ground black pepper

Chef and good friend Dave Rubell, from Los Angeles, showed me how to make these rolls when he visited. His clients adore them as ours do now. Balsamic syrup is found at some supermarkets and at specialty food stores, particularly those specialising in Italian products. It is a treacle-like version of balsamic vinegar.

Method

Roll out a piece of plastic wrap, about 40 cm long, onto a flat work surface.

Lay out prosciutto slices onto plastic wrap, making a rectangle 30 cm x 20 cm. Fill any gaps with small pieces of prosciutto.

Spread a thin layer of mayonnaise over prosciutto. Make a line of rocket along the length of prosciutto, 4 cm in from the edge closest to you. Scatter Parmesan over rocket and top with fig slices running lengthwise along rocket.

Drizzle a pencil-thin line of balsamic syrup over figs and season with pepper.

Starting from the edge closest to you, roll prosciutto over figs as tightly as possible. Continue to roll till fully wrapped and filling is tightly encased. It should resemble sushi.

Wrap in plastic wrap and refrigerate till required or for up to 2 days.

When ready to serve, neaten ends using a sharp knife. Slice roll into 2 cm thick pieces. Place pieces cut-side up on a platter. Drizzle each prosciutto roll with a drop of balsamic syrup and serve immediately.

Ricotta and Pesto Torte

**Makes one x 1 litre
(4 cup) bowl**

90 g (½ cup) sun-dried cherry tomatoes or sliced sun-dried tomatoes (drained of oil)

65 g (½ cup) lightly toasted pine nuts

350 g cream cheese (do not use spreadable or low fat)

200 g ricotta

175 g unsalted butter (melted but not boiled, cooled)

100 g Basil Pesto (see page 150)

100 g Sun-dried Tomato Pesto (see page 150)

After 15 years in existence this is still one of my most sought-after recipes. It appeared in my first book (which is now out of print). Serve as you would a dip at a party; it looks fabulous, everyone adores it, everyone wants the recipe. You cannot go wrong!

Method

Line a 1 litre (4-cup) bowl with plastic wrap. Place a circle of sun-dried tomatoes in the base of the bowl and cover the gaps with a single layer of pine nuts.

Chop cream cheese into cubes and allow cream cheese and ricotta to come to room temperature.

Into a food processor bowl fitted with a metal blade place cream cheese and process till smooth. Add melted butter and process till combined. Add ricotta and briefly pulse to combine. Remove mixture from processor and divide into 3, as the torte will have 3 layers.

Place the first layer of cream cheese mixture into the torte bowl and smooth with a small palette knife or spatula.

Cover the first layer with a thin layer of Basil Pesto and smooth. Sprinkle half the remaining pine nuts over the Basil Pesto. Spread and smooth a second layer of cream cheese mixture and cover this with a thin layer of Sun-dried Tomato Pesto. Sprinkle the rest of the pine nuts over the Sun-dried Tomato Pesto.

Spread and smooth the final layer of cream cheese mixture. Cover with plastic wrap and chill for at least 4 hours or for up to 3 days.

Unmould onto a serving platter and accompany with crostini, toast rounds, toasted pita crisps or crackers.

Barbecued Marinated Frenched Lamb Cutlets with Cucumber and Mint Relish

Makes 16 cocktail serves or 3–4 main serves

550 g–620 g (16) baby Frenched lamb cutlets (1 Frenched lamb rack will yield 8 cutlets)

½ recipe Mixed Herb and Garlic Rub

1 tbsp olive oil for greasing barbecue

flaky sea salt and freshly ground black pepper

Cucumber and Mint Relish (see page 165)

Mixed Herb and Garlic Rub

Makes 80 g

1 tbsp black peppercorns

1½ tsp flaky sea salt

2 large cloves garlic (peeled)

1 small red chilli (finely chopped)

2 tbsp + 1 tsp finely chopped thyme leaves

2 tbsp + 1 tsp finely chopped sage leaves

2 tbsp + 1 tsp finely chopped parsley leaves

30 ml (2 tbsp) olive oil

extra olive oil (if storing)

Particularly in summer it may suit you to barbecue nibbles to serve with drinks. The aroma of barbecuing lamb with herbs will certainly draw guests outside.

Method

Place cutlets into a non-reactive bowl, add Mixed Herb and Garlic Rub and massage it into cutlets. Leave to marinate for 4 hours or overnight in the refrigerator.

Preheat barbecue flat plate, making sure you have a high heat. (Alternatively heat a heavy-based frying pan or grill plate on the stovetop.) Smear olive oil on barbecue and wipe off residue with paper towels so that the flat plate is oiled but virtually dry.

Place cutlets onto flat plate and, for baby-sized Frenched lamb cutlets, cook for 3 minutes on each side or till medium–rare.

Remove cutlets from heat, place onto a warmed tray, cover with a heavy tea towel and rest at room temperature for 5 minutes.

Season to taste and serve hot or warm with Cucumber and Mint Relish.

This rub also works well on pork or venison.

To make Mixed Herb and Garlic Rub

Place peppercorns, salt and garlic into a mortar and pound with a pestle till crushed.

Add chilli, thyme, sage and parsley and pound till crushed and combined.

Add half of the oil and mix well. Drizzle remaining oil into herbs while mixing and pounding.

Use immediately or, if storing, place into a small container and pack down firmly. Pour on a little olive oil to coat, rub and then cover with a tight-fitting lid. Refrigerate for up to 5 days. When ready to use, stir well.

Chicken Tulips in Red- and Blackcurrant Marinade

Makes 16 cocktail serves	Red- and Blackcurrant Marinade	15 ml (1 tbsp) Kikkoman soy sauce	2 tsp finely grated orange zest
800 g (16) chicken tulips (or 8 large chicken wings)	Yields 160 ml	2 tsp Dijon mustard	½ tsp freshly ground black pepper
Red- and Blackcurrant Marinade	85 ml (⅓ cup) redcurrant jelly	1 clove crushed garlic	
flaky sea salt and freshly ground black pepper	37 g (¼ cup) destalked blackcurrants (roughly chopped) (if frozen, thawed)	15 ml (1 tbsp) sherry vinegar	

Make plenty of these deliciously sticky chicken pass-arounds as guests love them. A chicken tulip looks like a tiny drumstick; it is a chicken wing cut into two with the meat pulled inside out. If tulips are not available, use chicken wings.

Method
Place chicken tulips (or chicken wings) into a non-reactive bowl. Add marinade and massage well into chicken.

Refrigerate for 4 hours or preferably overnight as the longer marination will develop the flavour.

Preheat barbecue flat plate (or heavy-based frying pan) to medium–hot.

To protect the cooking surface from the sticky marinade, line flat plate with a Teflon sheet. Drain chicken of excess marinade and discard marinade.

Place tulips (wings) on one half of Teflon sheet and cover chicken with the other half.

Cook chicken for 7–10 minutes till well browned. Turn chicken tulips over, cover with Teflon, and cook for a further 7–10 minutes till chicken is well browned all over and cooked through.

Remove chicken tulips from barbecue onto a warm tray. Cover with aluminium foil and rest at room temperature for 3–5 minutes.

Season to taste and serve hot or warm.

To make Red-and Blackcurrant Marinade
Place all ingredients into a small bowl and whisk to combine.

Store Red- and Blackcurrant Chicken Marinade in refrigerator for up to 1 week.

Barbecued Flatbreads with Sun-dried Tomato Pesto

Makes 10

250 ml (1 cup) warm water

1½ tsp Fermipan yeast (this fast-acting yeast powder is available at many supermarkets)

½ tsp liquid honey

280 g (2 cups) high grade flour

1 tsp flaky sea salt

½ tsp toasted and ground cumin seeds

¼ tsp freshly ground black pepper

15 ml (1 tbsp) olive oil

Sun-dried Tomato Pesto (see page 150)

olive oil for greasing barbecue

Well-known Wellingtonian Alick Shaw, ex-chef and former deputy mayor, gave me this recipe. I loved these breads when he barbecued them for his guests while dinner was cooking.

Method

In a jug place water, yeast and honey, and mix together with a fork.

Place flour, salt, cumin and pepper into bowl of a food processor fitted with a metal blade, and pulse to combine. Add yeast mixture and pulse till dough just begins to form a ball.

Tip dough onto a lightly floured work surface and knead till it is a smooth, well-worked ball.

Break into 10 even portions and roll into 10 smooth round balls.

Lightly grease a low-sided baking tray with oil or baking spray and place dough balls onto tray. Cover lightly with a greased piece of plastic wrap and leave balls to rise for 30–40 minutes or till balls are double in volume. (Alternatively, dough balls can be placed in refrigerator overnight. Bring out of refrigerator 2 hours before required to allow them to come to room temperature and then leave to rise till double the volume they were the previous day.)

Preheat barbecue flat plate to medium-hot. Smear barbecue with oil and rub off residue with a paper towel so the flat plate is virtually dry.

Pat out each ball to a 10 cm round. Place half a teaspoon of Sun-dried Tomato Pesto onto one-half of each round, fold over second half and pinch to join two halves.

Place onto preheated barbecue plate and barbecue for 2–3 minutes on each side or till pale golden brown.

Remove from barbecue and serve warm.

Warm Olives with Winter Herbs

Makes 1¼ cups

285 g olives (assorted colours and sizes, with stones in, in brine)

190 ml (¾ cup) extra virgin olive oil

several sprigs of fresh rosemary, thyme and savory

small pinch of Sicilian red pepper flakes

¼ tsp freshly grated lemon zest

For drinks it's always handy to have a batch of marinated olives in the refrigerator. The larger the variety of olives, the more interesting the bowl will appear. These olives will become more fragrant with time.

Method

Remove olives from brine and rinse under cold water.

Place olives, oil, herbs, pepper flakes and lemon zest into a non-reactive pot set over a low heat and heat till just warm. Let sit at room temperature for 6 hours or in the refrigerator for up to 3 months.

To serve, warm olives in their oil in a small pot set over a low heat. Drain olives from oil into a serving bowl, reserving oil for use in a dressing or to toss through pasta. If you wish, retain herbs for garnish.

Chilli-spiced Almonds with Cumin

Makes 500 g or 12 aperitif serves

1½ tsp flaky sea salt

1½ tsp ground cumin seeds

1 tsp hot chilli flakes (buy as flakes or finely chop 2–3 small dried chillies)

1 small fresh chilli (finely chopped)

10 g (1 tbsp) sugar

45 ml (3 tbsp) peanut oil

360 g (2⅓ cups) blanched almonds

125 g (½ cup + 2½ tbsp) sugar

Chef Michael Lee-Richards first gave me the recipe for these sweet and spicy, very addictive nuts. Store in an airtight container in the pantry for up to two weeks.

Method

Lightly grease a low-sided baking tray with baking spray or oil.

Place salt, cumin seeds, chilli flakes, fresh chilli and first measure of sugar into a bowl and mix together.

Place oil in a heavy-based frying pan over a medium heat till hot. Add almonds and sprinkle second measure of sugar over almonds. Cook almonds for 8–12 minutes, stirring from time to time, till they become golden and sugar has caramelised.

Remove almonds from pan and add to bowl with spices. Stir together quickly to ensure spices are spread evenly over almonds.

Pour almonds onto prepared tray and before they are completely cool break into pieces. Once cold, store in an airtight container.

Lavender Lemonade

Makes 1.8 litres syrup

6 Meyer lemons

300 g (1½ cups) sugar

1.25 litres (5 cups) water

¼ cup chopped fresh English lavender leaves

560 ml (2¼ cups) lemon juice

lavender flowers to garnish

Always use English lavender (*Lavandula augustifolia or L. intermedia*) as opposed to French lavender for culinary purposes to avoid the pronounced lavender aroma common in toiletries. Guests who are not drinking alcohol really appreciate an interesting and refreshing drink.

Method

Peel lemons with a sharp peeler so there is as little white pith as possible on the peel (in other words leaving as much white pith on the lemon as possible).

Cut lemons in half and extract juice.

Roughly chop peel (zest) and place in food processor bowl fitted with a metal blade. Add sugar and process till zest is finely chopped.

Place zest and sugar, water and lavender leaves in a non-reactive pot set over a low heat and stir till sugar is dissolved.

Increase heat and bring syrup to a boil. Reduce heat and simmer for 5 minutes. Place a lid onto pot and cool. Strain syrup through a fine sieve, preferably lined with muslin. Discard zest and lavender leaves. Add lemon juice and stir.

Store in refrigerator in a sealed container for up to 2 months. Dilute syrup usually to a ratio of ⅓ syrup to ⅔ water or soda water, but dilution depends on flavour and ripeness of lemons. Serve with ice and lavender garnish.

Falafel with Yoghurt, Feta and Dill Dressing

Makes 28 cocktail-size portions

65 ml (¼ cup) water

100 g (½ cup) bulgur wheat

15 ml (1 tbsp) olive oil

125 g (1 medium) red onion (finely diced)

2 cloves garlic (finely chopped)

¼ tsp crushed red chilli flakes

1¼ tsp cumin seeds (toasted and crushed in a mortar with a pestle)

1¼ tsp coriander seeds (toasted and crushed in a mortar with a pestle)

220 g (1½ cups) canned chickpeas (drained, or soaked, cooked and drained dried chickpeas)

30 ml (2 tbsp) lemon juice

35 g (¼ cup) pine nuts

25 g (4) sun-dried tomatoes (finely chopped)

2 tbsp finely chopped coriander leaves

2 tbsp finely chopped parsley leaves

1 tbsp finely chopped chives

flaky sea salt

freshly ground black pepper

oil for barbecuing

Yoghurt, Feta and Dill Dressing (see page 158)

Generally falafel are deep-fried but I like to barbecue them as they taste fresher and lighter. Make larger falafel and serve between Barbecued Flatbreads with Sun-dried Tomato Pesto (see page 150).

Method

Place water in a small pot and bring to the boil over medium heat. Remove from heat and add bulgur wheat. Cover with a lid and leave to sit for 20 minutes, or till water is absorbed and wheat has softened.

Pour olive oil into a small, heavy-based pan, set over a medium heat and when hot add onion. Cook for 2–3 minutes or till softened. Add garlic and cook for a further 2–3 minutes till onion and garlic are translucent but not browned.

Add chilli flakes, freshly ground cumin and coriander seeds and cook for 1 minute. Remove from heat and cool.

In a bowl of a food processor fitted with a metal blade, place bulgur wheat, onion mixture, chickpeas, lemon juice, pine nuts, sun-dried tomatoes, chopped coriander, parsley and chives, with salt and pepper to taste. Pulse till roughly chopped and mixture is combined.

Rest mixture for 15 minutes in refrigerator before forming into 28 even-sized balls. Lightly flatten to about the size of a 50-cent coin.

Preheat barbecue flat plate, cover with Teflon sheet, or alternatively brush with a generous layer of oil. Cook falafel on preheated barbecue for 2–3 minutes on each side till golden brown and heated through. Remove from barbecue and, if required, keep warm by covering with aluminium foil. Serve warm with Yoghurt, Feta and Dill Dressing.

Basil's Ginger Beer Battered Fish with Cashew Dipping Sauce

Serves 4–6, or makes 12–24 finger-food-size pieces

140 g (1 cup) flour

14 g (2 tbsp) cornflour

½ tsp baking powder

½ tsp flaky sea salt

315 ml (1¼ cups) ginger beer

2 egg whites (lightly whisked)

3 tbsp finely chopped Italian parsley leaves

70 g (½ cup) flour (seasoned with flaky sea salt and freshly ground black pepper)

450 g firm fish such as groper (hapuka) or blue

cod cut into 12–24 even-sized pieces

canola or grapeseed oil for deep frying

lemon or lime wedges

flaky sea salt and freshly ground black pepper

Cashew Dipping Sauce (see page 166)

Several years ago, Basil Wairau, who was head chef at one of Wellington's busiest cafés gave me his recipe for ginger beer batter handwritten on a paper napkin. Always make more portions of fish than you think you will need. Go all out and accompany with Homemade Chips (see page 43).

Method
In a medium-size bowl place flour, cornflour, baking powder and salt and combine. Make a well in centre of flour mixture and pour in ginger beer. Whisk batter till smooth.

Gently fold in egg whites till just combined.

Place Italian parsley onto a small plate. Place seasoned flour on a second plate. Dip fish into Italian parsley to cover on all sides, then into seasoned flour.

Pour oil to half-fill a medium-size, heavy-based pot and set over a medium heat. Heat oil till hot. Test heat by dropping half a teaspoon of batter into oil. If it sizzles and rises to the surface the oil is hot enough to deep-fry in.

In small batches dip herbed and floured fish pieces into Ginger Beer Batter and place immediately into pot.

Cook for 3–4 minutes or till batter is golden and fish is cooked through. Cooking time will depend on the thickness and size of fish pieces.

Using a Japanese brass wire skimmer remove fish from pot onto a tray lined with paper towels.

While the second and third batches of fish are being cooked (and if the first batch hasn't been eaten!), keep fish warm by spreading out onto a baking tray lined with paper towels. Leave uncovered and place in a 150 °C oven for up to 5 minutes.

Serve with lemon or lime wedges, season with salt and pepper and accompany with Cashew Dipping Sauce.

Saffron Crepes with Roasted Pumpkin and Cumin

Serves 10

olive oil

520 g (small wedge) Crown pumpkin (skinned, seeded and sliced into 5 mm slices)

1 tsp cumin seeds (toasted and ground)

250 g (1 cup) cream cheese (softened)

10 ml (2 tsp) lemon juice

10 Saffron Crepes

1 tsp cumin seeds (toasted)

32 g (4 tbsp) pistachio nuts (toasted and roughly chopped)

530 g–580 g (4 small) red capsicums (roasted, peeled and sliced)

flaky sea salt and freshly ground black pepper

2 large handfuls baby rocket leaves

Saffron Crepes

Makes 10

125 ml (½ cup) milk

125 ml (½ cup) water

2 eggs

¼ tsp flaky sea salt

140 g (1 cup) flour

20 g (2 tbsp) butter (melted)

2–3 saffron threads (lightly toasted and lightly crushed)

20 g (2 tbsp) butter (diced)

This recipe needs to be thought through as two steps. First step is to make the crepes; second step is to fill them. Unfilled or filled crepes can be stored in the refrigerator overnight. If time is a problem for you, then adopt a DIY method and place bowls of ingredients in front of guests and let them fill their own crepes.

Method
Preheat oven to 200 ºC.

Lightly grease a low-sided tray with olive oil. Place pumpkin on tray and sprinkle with ground cumin. Place in oven and bake for 10–12 minutes till pumpkin is fork-tender and slightly coloured. Cool.

Place cream cheese and lemon juice into a bowl and mix to a smooth consistency.

On a clean board or benchtop lay out the crepes. Spread half of each crepe with 1½–2 tablespoons cream cheese mixture per crepe.

Sprinkle cumin seeds and pistachios over cream cheese.

On top of cream cheese place 2 slices of pumpkin and 4–6 slices of red capsicum. Season with salt and pepper.

Top with rocket and fold second half of crepe over the top.

Serve warm, at room temperature or cold. For warm crepes, place crepes onto baking tray(s), cover with aluminium foil and place in 190 ºC oven for 7–10 minutes till heated through.

To make Saffron Crepes
Place milk, water, eggs, salt, flour and butter in a food processor fitted with a metal blade. Process for 20 seconds till smooth, scraping down sides if needed. Pour into a bowl and stir in saffron.

Cover batter and chill for at least 2 hours or overnight.

Heat a 15 cm crepe pan till hot. Place a knob of butter in the pan and swirl to coat pan. Remove pan from heat and wipe out excess butter using paper towels.

Mediterranean Feta and Herb Dip

Serves 8–10

150 g creamy-style feta

115 g (½ cup) sour cream

1½ tsp toasted fennel seeds (lightly crushed)

1 tbsp sliced mint leaves

1 tbsp finely chopped chives

10 ml (2 tsp) lemon juice

flaky sea salt and freshly ground black pepper

Gently stir batter and add enough batter to very thinly coat bottom of pan, swirling to coat evenly. You are aiming for a paper-thin crepe. Pour excess back into bowl. Return to heat and cook till lacy and brown. Flip crepe and cook on other side till lightly browned.

Transfer crepe to a tray and repeat till all batter is used.

Cool and proceed with Saffron Crepes with Roasted Pumpkin and Cumin or alternatively, when cool, place on plastic-wrap-lined trays (if stacking, place plastic wrap between), cover with plastic wrap and store in refrigerator for up to 2 days.

If you are inexperienced at making crepes, double the batter mixture as the first 2 or 3 you cook may not be perfect — but practice does make perfect.

Serve with crudités (choose 3 or 4 vegetables from an assortment of cauliflower florets, celery and carrot sticks, radishes, sliced fennel bulb or cherry tomatoes), plain crackers or toasted pita crisps. Slather leftover dip on toast at breakfast and top with sliced tomatoes and basil leaves.

Method

Place feta and sour cream into a medium-sized bowl and, using a large fork, stir together till mixture is a chunky mash.

Add fennel seeds, mint, chives and lemon juice with salt and pepper to taste. Stir in with a fork till ingredients are well combined but feta remains lumpy.

Cover dip and place in refrigerator for 3–4 hours for flavours to develop or, better still, overnight. Store in refrigerator for up to 4 days.

Clockwise from top left:

Mediterranean Feta and Herb Dip (see page 29)

Herbed Scampi Tails with Citrus Crème Fraîche

Saffron Crepes with Roasted Pumpkin and Cumin (see page 28)

Herbed Scampi Tails with Citrus Crème Fraîche

Serves 8

300–480 g (16) scampi tails (deveined, peeled of shell but leaving very end of tail intact)

1 tbsp finely chopped Italian parsley leaves

1 tsp finely grated lemon zest

½ tsp flaky sea salt

¼ tsp freshly ground black pepper

15 ml (1 tbsp) olive oil

Citrus Crème Fraîche (see page 161)

As an expression of luxury serve this delicacy with drinks. You will find New Zealand scampi, always sold as a frozen product, at selected seafood shops. If your retailer doesn't stock them plead to have scampi ordered in for you.

Method

Preheat oven to 200 °C or preheat barbecue to medium–hot.

Into a medium-size bowl place scampi tails, parsley, lemon zest, salt, pepper and olive oil. Toss scampi to coat evenly.

Spread scampi tails onto a low-sided baking tray with approximately 1 cm space between. Place into preheated oven and cook for 3–4 minutes only or till flesh is white. Alternatively place scampi tails onto preheated barbecue flat plate and cook for 1–2 minutes on each side.

Serve warm or at room temperature with Citrus Crème Fraîche. Alternatively refrigerate to serve cold.

TWO

SUMMER

Eating outside, whether on a tiny deck overlooking a myriad of apartments, in a back yard under the clothesline, or indeed in a luxurious garden, everyone feels hungrier. Summer entertaining can be so simple: fish fillets tossed in herbs and oil, barbecued and served with flaky sea salt and lemon for starters; barbecued rib-eye steaks, minted Jersey Benne potatoes, tomatoes sliced with basil, green beans drizzled with lemon oil and Buttercrunch lettuce salad for main course; and raspberries in champagne with lemon zest or strawberries tossed in balsamic syrup for dessert. Sometimes, though, you need that special salad, an outstanding dessert or the best version of hamburger and chips to lift your ante on summer entertaining.

Breakfast Salad

Serves 4

300 g (12) rashers rindless middle bacon (grilled till crispy)

1 small–medium Iceberg lettuce (outer leaves discarded, torn into chunky bite-sized pieces)

4 handfuls rocket leaves

4 tomatoes (quartered) or 8 cherry tomatoes (halved)

½ recipe Caesar Salad Dressing (see page 155)

8 large eggs (poached)

1 avocado (stone removed, peeled and cut into quarters)

80 g Parmesan cheese (shaved)

½ tsp flaky sea salt

¼ tsp freshly ground black pepper

This salad with Iceberg lettuce, crispy bacon, avocado, poached eggs and Parmesan is my absolute favourite summer brunch dish. I began loving it after eating a version of it at Bambina, a café in Ponsonby, Auckland. If you prefer, dress the salad with simple olive oil and balsamic dressing rather than Caesar dressing.

Method

Cut or break 8 rashers grilled bacon into chunky pieces. Reserve remaining 4 rashers whole.

Into a large bowl place lettuce, rocket, tomatoes and chopped bacon. Toss together.

Divide lettuce mixture between 4 pasta-style bowls. Drizzle each serve with 1 tablespoon Caesar Salad Dressing. Top each serve with 2 poached eggs.

Cut each quarter avocado into two or three and place beside eggs. Drizzle each serve with another 1 tablespoon Caesar Dressing.

Divide shaved Parmesan among serves, scattering on top of eggs. Top each serving with a bacon rasher and season with salt and pepper. Serve immediately.

To poach eggs

Use freshest eggs possible (preferably free range or organic). Over a high heat bring a large pan of hot water to a rolling boil and then reduce heat to simmer. When water is simmering break egg on the firm edge of a bench close to the pan and pour egg into pan. Repeat with remaining eggs but do not overcrowd the pan. When whites are cooked and yolks are firmish but still runny remove from pan using a fish slice.

Corn-fed Chicken and Herbed Lentil Salad

Serves 4

400 g (2) corn-fed chicken single breasts (skin on)

15 ml (1 tbsp) olive oil

1 tsp flaky sea salt

½ tsp freshly ground black pepper

30 ml (2 tbsp) lemon juice

30 ml (2 tbsp) extra virgin olive oil

2 tbsp finely chopped chives

flaky sea salt and freshly ground black pepper

Herbed Lentil Salad

Herbed Lentil Salad

Serves 4

15 ml (1 tbsp) olive oil

90 g (½ small) onion (finely diced)

1 small clove garlic (crushed)

80 g (1 medium) carrot (diced)

1 sprig thyme

1 bay leaf

½ tsp dried aniseed (crushed)

140 g green lentils

½ tsp flaky sea salt

500 ml (2 cups) cold water

30 ml (2 tbsp) extra virgin olive oil

Enjoy this casual but extremely flavoursome fork-food dish at lunch or dinner. Corn-fed chicken is always plump and juicy.

Method

Preheat oven to 220 °C.

Place chicken into a bowl with first measure of oil, sprinkle with salt and pepper and toss together.

Place chicken on a low-sided baking tray skin-side up and place in oven. Cook for 15–20 minutes or till chicken juices run clear. Test by inserting a metal skewer into thickest part of chicken breast.

Cover tray with aluminium foil for up to 20 minutes to allow chicken to rest.

Don kitchen gloves as the chicken will be hot, and using hands, remove chicken skin, then shred chicken. If you wish, snip chicken skin into pieces with scissors, place back onto baking tray and place in oven. Roast for 10–15 minutes or till crispy.

Place shredded chicken into a bowl; add lemon juice, extra virgin olive oil and chives. Stir to combine and moisten with any residue juices from chicken baking tray. Season to taste.

Place Herbed Lentil Salad onto a large platter, or divide amongst individual plates, and top with warm chicken. If you wish, top chicken with crispy chicken skin.

To make Herbed Lentil Salad

Into a medium-size, heavy-based pot pour oil, and heat to medium–hot.

Reduce heat to medium, add onion and cook for 2 minutes or till onion is beginning to soften. Add garlic, carrot, thyme, bay leaf and aniseed. Cook for 5–6 minutes or till onion is soft.

Add lentils, first measure of salt, and pour in water.

Over a medium heat cook for 20–25 minutes till lentils are soft to the bite but not mushy, and most of the water has been absorbed. Drain off excess water.

Potato and Chorizo Salad

1 tsp balsamic vinegar

10 ml (2 tsp) lemon juice

flaky sea salt to taste

¼ tsp freshly ground black pepper

2 tbsp finely chopped chives

2 tbsp finely chopped Italian parsley leaves

Serves 6

120 g chorizo sausage (thickly sliced and if large rounds, cut into quarters)

600 g new potatoes (Jersey Bennes are ideal) (cut into large chunks, simmered in water with a little salt till fork-tender then drained)

30 ml (2 tbsp) lemon juice

110 g (12–14) cherry tomatoes (if possible red and yellow, halved)

21 g (3 tbsp) pine nuts (lightly toasted)

14–16 mint leaves (roughly torn)

Chilli Saffron Vinaigrette (see page 156)

flaky sea salt and freshly ground black pepper

Remove from heat and remove thyme and bay leaf.

Add extra virgin olive oil, balsamic vinegar and lemon juice and season to taste.

Add chives and parsley and stir to combine. Serve warm or at room temperature.

Use Puy lentils imported from France, or you will find very good green lentils imported from Canada at organic shops. Aniseed is an anise-flavoured herb. If you have trouble finding this dried herb, substitute chopped fresh tarragon or chervil leaves.

Serve warm with simple barbecued fish, salmon or lamb and, if you wish, accompany with barbecued red capsicum halves.

Method

Place a frying pan over a medium heat and when hot add chorizo and brown on both sides.

In a large bowl place warm potatoes and lemon juice and gently toss to coat. Add tomatoes, chorizo, pine nuts and mint.

Pour dressing over potatoes and toss well to combine ingredients. Season wit salt and pepper.

Preferably serve warm but it is also very good served cold.

Photographs on following pages: Corn-fed Chicken and Herbed Lentil Salad; Potato and Chorizo Salad

Classic Hamburgers

Serves 6

olive oil for barbecue

6 JG Hamburger Patties

120 g Monterey Jack cheese (or similar; a semi-soft cheese with a mild flavour and ability to slowly melt) (thinly sliced

and cut into squares to fit the burger patties)

6 hamburger buns (aim for flattish buns around 8 cm diameter, cut in half through the centre)

125 ml (½ cup) Mustard Mayonnaise (see page 153)

90 g finely shredded Iceberg lettuce (about ¼ of an Iceberg lettuce)

Homemade Chips (see page 43)

Zucchini Pickle (see page 163)

I ate the most perfect hamburger of my life in the bar Jean Georges, a very upscale, contemporary-style French restaurant and bar, on the fourth floor at Three on the Bund in Shanghai. I was overwhelmed by the simplicity of the ingredients when Chef Eric Johnson kindly rattled them off. Trust me, the patties are only minced meat and seasoning. You must visit your butcher to buy the meat ingredients.

Method
Preheat barbecue flat plate to medium hot. Brush with oil and wipe off any residue.

Place JG Hamburger Patties directly from refrigerator onto preheated barbecue. Cook for 4–5 minutes on first side, turn over and cook for 2–3 minutes on the second side. Place cheese on the patties and cook for a further 1–2 minutes. Patties should be golden brown on each side, slightly pink in the centre and cheese just beginning to melt.

To rest patties, remove from barbecue onto a warmed tray. Rest a sheet of Teflon on patties so that cheese does not stick to tea towel and tightly cover with a tea towel.

To assemble Classic Hamburgers
Place 6 hamburger bun bases on a tray (if buns feel a little stale, lightly toast buns on either side). Place tops on a second tray. Spread cut side of buns with 2 teaspoons each of Mustard Mayonnaise.

Divide lettuce among bun bases.

Place a hamburger pattie on top of lettuce and close with bun top.

Serve with freshly made Homemade Chips and accompany with Zucchini Pickle and, if you wish, mustard and tomato sauce.

JG Hamburger Patties

Makes 6 patties

310 g lean beef brisket
(chopped into 4 cm dice)

310 g beef chuck steak
(chopped into 3 cm dice)

1 tsp flaky sea salt

155 g brisket fat (white and
firm) (roughly chopped)

85 g rindless smoked
bacon (roughly chopped)

1¾ tsp toasted and freshly
ground cumin seeds

1 tsp freshly ground black
pepper

To make JG Hamburger Patties

Place brisket and chuck steak into a ceramic dish and sprinkle all over with salt. Leave to sit in refrigerator overnight.

Set up a mincer with the largest hole (5 mm) attachment. (If you do not have a mincer, you may be able to convince your butcher to salt and mince the meat cuts for you. An extremely second-best option would be to mince the meat in batches using the pulse button on food processor.) Feed salted beef, fat and bacon through the mincer.

Change mincer attachment to the next smallest hole (4 mm) and feed minced meat through again. Transfer mince to a large bowl.

Add cumin seeds and black pepper and mix well.

Divide mixture evenly into six, roll each portion into a ball and flatten to disc-shape 7.5 cm–8 cm diameter with 3 cm thickness. Neaten sides.

Cover and refrigerate patties for 1–2 hours, overnight, or for up to 2 days before cooking.

Photograph on following page: Classic Hamburgers and Homemade Chips

Homemade Chips

Serves 6

800 g (4) Agria potatoes
(peeled)

canola or grapeseed oil for
deep frying

flaky sea salt (if possible
the smoky version)

Many people say they never eat chips but as we all know most people simply adore them. There is nothing as good as chips you make yourself and this version allows you to do all the hard work ahead of time. Good chips always require precooking and then a second cooking. In this method the second cooking uses par-cooked chips which have been frozen.

Method

Cut potatoes into chips using a sharp knife. If you are serious about chips, an old-fashioned style chip cutter is a handy addition to the kitchen. Place chips between two clean tea towels to dry thoroughly.

Into a deep, wide-based pot that a chip basket will fit into, pour oil to approximately one-third full. Place pot over a medium heat and heat till hot. Test heat of oil by dropping a chip into oil. If chip sizzles and rises to the surface the oil is hot enough.

Place about a quarter of the chips into basket, and lower into hot oil.

Cook for 2–3 minutes or till chips are par-cooked. At this stage chips will not be golden.

Remove from oil, drain and tip chips onto a tray lined with paper towels. Chill till cold. Repeat this process till all the chips are par-cooked.

Transfer chips to a freezer-proof tray, cover with plastic wrap and freeze. This step is best done one day ahead or could be up to 10 days ahead.

When ready to serve reheat oil to hot. Test heat of oil by dropping in a chip as previously. Transfer about a quarter of the frozen chips to chip basket and lower into hot oil.

Deep fry for 2–3 minutes or till chips are crispy and golden brown on the outside. Drain and tip onto trays lined with paper towels.

Sprinkle with sea salt and serve immediately.

Photograph: Classic Hamburgers and Homemade Chips

Warm Pumpkin and Feta Salad

Serves 3–4 as a light lunch or 4–6 as an accompaniment

400 g Crown (grey-skinned) pumpkin (cut into batons 1 cm thick and 5 cm in length)

30 g (3 tbsp) butter

80 g (3) rindless bacon rashers (cut into thick strips)

115–125 g (18) French beans (topped, tailed, blanched and kept warm)

Raspberry Vinaigrette (see page 158)

110 g creamy-style feta (cut into cubes)

2 large handfuls rocket leaves

1½ tsp pink peppercorns in brine (drained, rinsed in cold water and roughly chopped)

The warmth of the bacon, pumpkin and beans in this salad will make a creamy feta particularly unctuous. Enjoy the salad as a stand-alone meal or as an accompaniment to roast leg of lamb, grilled fish or barbecued steak.

Method

Place pumpkin into steamer basket over a pot of simmering water and cook till just tender. Cooking time will vary according to ripeness and age of pumpkin. Remove from steamer and cool.

Place butter in a heavy-based frying pan, over a medium heat, and melt. Add bacon, tossing occasionally, till bacon has browned but is not crisp. Add pumpkin to pan, place a lid on pan for about 1 minute, and gently toss contents to heat through, being careful not to break the pumpkin.

Transfer bacon and pumpkin to a large bowl. Add beans and Raspberry Vinaigrette. Toss gently to just combine and gently place warm salad onto serving platter.

Scatter feta, rocket and pink peppercorns over the top and serve immediately.

Corn, Zucchini and Bulgur Wheat Salad

**Serves 5–6 or 10–12
when there is an array
of salads**

130 g (¾ cup) bulgur
wheat

1 litre (4 cups) boiling
water

2 corn cobs (blanched and
refreshed)

1 red chilli (deseeded and
finely chopped)

200 g (2) zucchini (finely
sliced lengthwise) (to slice
zucchini very finely use a
mandoline or Rex peeler)

70 g (½) red onion (finely
chopped)

¼ cup finely chopped dill

½ cup finely chopped
Italian parsley leaves

65 ml (¼ cup) lemon juice

65 ml (¼ cup) olive oil

1 tsp flaky sea salt

½ tsp freshly ground black
pepper

This summery salad, perfect with simple barbecued meals, takes care of starch and vegetables in one bowl. This is also the ideal salad when you need to take a salad to someone else's house.

Method

Place bulgur wheat into a large bowl and add boiling water. Stir, cover and set aside to soak for 45 minutes.

Drain through a large sieve, discarding water. Transfer bulgur wheat to a clean tea towel, wring to extract excess water and tip into a large bowl.

Slice kernels from corn cobs and add to bulgur wheat. Add chilli, zucchini, onion, dill and parsley.

Pour lemon juice and oil into a jug with salt and pepper. Whisk well. Pour dressing over bulgur wheat and vegetables, and toss ingredients together.

Cover salad with plastic wrap and refrigerate for one hour or overnight for flavours to develop, or keep for up to 3 days.

Serve chilled or remove from refrigerator for 30–60 minutes to serve at room temperature.

Strawberry and Rhubarb Shortcake

Serves 4–6

100 g rhubarb (sliced in half lengthwise and then cut into 5 mm dice)

100 g strawberries (hulled and quartered)

40 g (3 tbsp + 1 tsp) brown sugar

80g (8 tbsp) white sugar

225 g (1 cup + ½ cup + 2 tbsp) flour

¼ tsp salt

2 tsp baking powder

75 g unsalted butter (chilled and diced)

finely grated zest of 1 orange

190 ml (¾ cup) cream, plus extra for brushing dough

whipped cream for serving (optional)

I call this a knock-up dessert; you can throw it together while the potatoes are cooking. Freshly baked always tastes best but if the need arises, reheat to serve.

Method

Preheat oven to 190 °C. Line a baking tray with baking paper and lightly grease with baking spray or melted butter.

To make the filling, into a small bowl place rhubarb, strawberries, 2 tablespoons brown sugar, 2 tablespoons white sugar and 2 tablespoons flour. Stir to combine.

To make the dough, place remaining flour, salt and baking powder into the bowl of a food processor fitted with a metal blade. Add butter and process till mixture resembles breadcrumbs. Alternatively, you could do this by hand.

Add zest, 1 teaspoon brown sugar and 5 tablespoons white sugar (this leaves 1 tablespoon of each sugar for topping) and using pulse button on food processor, mix till it is just combined.

With food processor running, working quickly, pour cream through the feed tube and process till dough just begins to form a ball.

Tip dough onto a lightly floured bench and gently mould into a ball. Divide ball in half.

On a lightly floured work surface roll out one half to a 17 cm round. This becomes the base. Slide the base onto the prepared tray and top with filling, leaving a 1 cm edge around, the outside. Brush this edge with cream.

Roll remaining dough out to a 19 cm round, slide a baking tray under it and then slide round on top of filling. Gently press base and top edges together to prevent fruit juices from seeping out while cooking.

To make the topping, into a small bowl place remaining brown sugar and white sugar. Brush top with cream and sprinkle with topping.

Place into preheated oven and cook for 25–30 minutes or till dough is cooked and top is lightly browned.

Remove from oven and serve warm. Accompany with whipped cream if you wish.

Rum Raisins

Serves 6–10

300 g raisins

water for covering raisins

300 g sugar

120 ml water

120 ml dark rum

1 tbsp finely grated lemon zest

Rum Raisins are a handy standby to serve as is, or with anything chocolatey or creamy. Serve alongside Baked Chocolate and Amaretto Cheesecake (see page 52).

Method

Wash raisins in cold water to remove any stalks or grit. Place in a small saucepan and cover with cold water.

Set over a medium heat, bring to the boil and cook for 5 minutes or till raisins are plump and juicy.

Strain, discard water and rinse raisins under cold water.

In a clean saucepan over a medium heat place sugar and water, and stir till dissolved. Bring to the boil and cook for 4–5 minutes till syrupy consistency is achieved.

Remove from heat, cool slightly, add rum, raisins and lemon zest and combine. Store in refrigerator for up to 3 months.

Raspberries with Crème de Cassis

Serves 8–10

500 g raspberries

32 g (4 tbsp) icing sugar

30 ml (2 tbsp) Crème de Cassis

Serve as a simple stand-alone dessert in pretty glasses or use as an accompaniment to anything featuring chocolate or lemon.

Method

Pile raspberries in a large bowl, sieve icing sugar over the top and pour in cassis.

Gently toss to coat raspberries.

Leave to macerate at room temperature for 1–2 hours.

Clockwise from above:

Rum Raisins

Raspberries with Crème de Cassis

Baked Chocolate and Amaretto Cheesecake (see page 52)

Baked Chocolate and Amaretto Cheesecake

Serves 8–12

220 g (1 packet) dark chocolate digestive biscuits

80 g (6–7) plain digestive biscuits

120 g unsalted butter (melted but not boiled)

100 g dark (70%) chocolate (buttons or tablet, chopped)

750 g cream cheese (at room temperature) (not easy spread or low fat)

200 g (1 cup) sugar

3 eggs

30 ml (2 tbsp) Amaretto (almond liqueur)

In this century if you are going to eat cheesecake it has to be worth every calorie and the good news is that this recipe is worth every calorie. Serve with Whole Poached Plums (page 55), Rum Raisins (page 50) or Raspberries with Crème de Cassis (page 50).

Method

Preheat oven to 160 °C.

Place chocolate digestive biscuits and plain digestive biscuits into bowl of a food processor fitted with a metal blade. Process till biscuits are crumbed.

Pour melted butter into biscuit crumbs and process till well combined.

Press crumb mixture onto base and sides of a 20 cm diameter spring-form (or loose-bottomed) 6 cm deep cake tin. Bring crumbs three-quarters of the way up the sides of the tin. Set base by placing in refrigerator or freezer while you make the filling, or overnight.

Place chocolate into a bowl and sit bowl over a pot one-quarter filled with water. Use a pot the bowl fits snugly into. Simmer on a gentle heat till chocolate is just melted. Remove from heat and stir till chocolate is entirely melted.

Place cream cheese and sugar into the bowl of a food processor fitted with a metal blade. Using pulse button process till smooth. You may need to scrape down the sides halfway through the process. Do not over-mix, as the cream cheese will break down and become runny which will make the cheesecake crack during baking. Add eggs, one at a time, processing between each addition.

Remove 1½ cups of cream cheese mixture and place into a bowl. Add melted chocolate and stir till completely combined. Set aside.

Add Amaretto to the mixture remaining in the food processor and pulse to combine. Pour half of the Amaretto cream cheese mixture into prepared tin. Spoon half of

Barbecued Fresh Figs with Creamy Blue Cheese

Serves 8

8 fresh ripe figs

olive oil

160 g creamy blue cheese (rind removed and sliced into 8)

20 g (8) walnuts (lightly toasted)

30 g (2½ tbsp) lightly flavoured floral honey such as Tawari honey

the chocolate mixture on top and, using a skewer, swirl the two mixtures together. Repeat with remaining mixtures. Do not smooth the top.

Place cheesecake into preheated oven and bake for 30–35 minutes till centre is bouncy to the touch and mixture wobbles when tin is gently shaken.

Remove cheesecake from oven and place directly onto bench to cool for at least 4 hours. Transfer cheesecake to refrigerator till it is completely cold, or preferably overnight.

To serve, remove sides from tin and slide cheesecake onto a serving platter ready to present or portion.

Secure new season walnuts and hijack figs while they are in season to serve for a simple but outstanding dessert.

Method

Preheat barbecue flat plate to a medium heat.

Trim stalk off each fig and cut through stalk end to halfway down. Make a second cut to make it appear as if the fig is cut in quarters.

Brush barbecue flat plate with oil and wipe off any residue.

Place figs onto barbecue, bottom-side first, and when lightly browned move figs to brown sides. Depending on size, ripeness and variety of figs, they should be browned, warmed through and yielding in 5–8 minutes.

Remove from barbecue to a platter and place a slice of creamy blue cheese in the cut part of each fig, followed by a walnut. Drizzle with a teaspoon of honey and serve warm.

Photograph on following page:

Barbecued Fresh Figs with Creamy Blue Cheese

Clockwise from top left:

Barbecued Fresh Figs with Creamy Blue Cheese (see page 53)

Whole Poached Plums

Lemon Frippery

Lemon Frippery

Serves 6

8 g (1 tbsp) gelatine

30 ml (2 tbsp) water

50 ml (3 tbsp + 1 tsp) sweet white wine (a dessert-style wine)

150 g (½ cup + 4 + ½ tbsp) caster sugar

finely grated zest 3 lemons

75 ml (5 tbsp) lemon juice

4 eggs (separated}

Wellington City Missioner and ex-chef, Father Des Britten, gave me this clever recipe. If you wish, serve with Raspberries with Crème de Cassis (see page 50).

Method

Sprinkle gelatine over water in a small bowl and leave for 5–10 minutes or till gelatine has absorbed water and become sponge like.

In a small pot place wine, sugar, lemon zest and juice and stir till combined. Place pot onto a low heat to warm only. Remove from heat, add gelatine and stir till sugar and gelatine are dissolved.

Whisk egg yolks till thick and light. Slowly pour warm gelatine mixture into egg yolks, whisking continuously. Beat egg whites till stiff peaks form and gently fold into egg yolk mixture. Pour mixture into a jug and three-quarters fill 6 x 290 ml wine glasses.

Chill for 2–4 hours till set. When set, a jelly will set on the base and a mousse-like froth will form on the top. Alternatively the mix will fill a 900 ml mould, which will require overnight setting.

Whole Poached Plums

Serves 8 as an accompaniment

400 g (2 cups) brown sugar

500 ml (2 cups) water

2 star anise

380–425 g (8) rich dark plums (we like to use Black Doris)

5 ml (1 tsp) Crème de Cassis

Poached Plums are an excellent foil to rich creamy desserts or the ideal accompaniment to muesli at brunch.

Method

Into a medium-size pot place sugar and water. Place over a medium heat and stir till sugar is dissolved. Add star anise and bring syrup to the boil. Add plums and to prevent plums from bobbing above the surface, place a single layer of greaseproof paper, cut into a round the same diameter as the pot, directly on top of fruit. Bring syrup back to the boil.

Reduce heat to a simmer and cook plums for 5–8 minutes or till tender but not soft. The cooking time will depend on the variety and the ripeness of the fruit. Plums will suddenly lose their shape if overcooked. Using a slotted spoon remove Poached Plums from liquid and transfer to a container. Cool. If you wish, remove split skins.

Leave remaining juices on the heat for 3–4 minutes to reduce slightly to a syrup. Add Crème de Cassis and pour into a jug to cool. Serve at room temperature.

THREE

WINTER

When the weather is too miserable for you to play outside take the opportunity to savour time in your own kitchen. Invite friends to your house to spend a mealtime together with roaring fire, fresh flowers and fogged-up windows. Prepare yourself though. Rug up on Saturday morning to visit your favourite food shops and spend the afternoon cooking up a storm. It's energising. Cook double the amount required so when you come home after battling a day at work, and the elements, you feel smug knowing that dinner is waiting for you.

Pork and Chicken Terrine with Dried Figs in Red Wine

Makes 1 terrine or 16–25 slices			
300–325 g (12–14) rindless streaky bacon slices	500 g chicken livers (trimmed of all sinew)	1 tbsp finely chopped sage leaves	1 tbsp flaky sea salt
500 g lean pork, shoulder or leg (cut into small dice)	100 g (7–10) shallots (peeled and finely chopped)	¾ tsp ground ginger	1 tsp freshly ground black pepper
250 g skinless chicken breast (roughly chopped)	3 tbsp finely chopped Italian parsley leaves	¾ tsp ground cinnamon	Dried Figs in Red Wine (see page 171)
	1 tbsp finely chopped thyme leaves	30 ml (2 tbsp) Madeira or dry sherry	
		15 ml (1 tbsp) brandy	

Today many people find a traditional French terrine too rich because of the added fat. This version is lighter than the traditional but still maintains great flavour. Serve as a lunch dish, a starter at dinner or as platter food with drinks.

Method
Preheat oven to 180 °C.

Line bases and sides of a 25 cm x 8 cm loaf tin or terrine dish with bacon slices leaving excess bacon hanging over sides of tin.

Into bowl of a food processor fitted with a metal blade place pork and process, using pulse button, till minced but minced unevenly. Transfer into a bowl.

Place chicken into the same food processor bowl and process to a consistency similar to pork. Tip chicken into bowl with pork.

Add chicken livers to bowl of food processor and process till finely minced. Tip into bowl with pork and chicken.

Add shallots, parsley, thyme, sage, ginger, cinnamon, Madeira and brandy, with salt and pepper to taste. Mix well. To check seasoning, roll a teaspoon of mixture into a ball and cook in microwave.

Spoon terrine mixture into bacon-lined tin. Fold excess bacon over to entirely cover top of terrine mixture.

Place terrine into preheated oven and cook for 1¼ to 1½ hours or till the juices run clear when pressed in the centre with the back of a spoon.

Remove terrine from oven and weight it down by placing a second loaf tin directly on top of terrine with a heavy object, for example a can of baked beans in the tin.

When cool, refrigerate weighted terrine overnight or for up to 3 days.

To serve, run a knife between tin and terrine. Invert onto board and remove terrine from tin. Serve with Dried Figs in Red Wine. Salad greens, little gherkins and sourdough bread are excellent add-ons also.

Creamy Mushrooms with Port

Serves 4

70 g (7 tbsp) unsalted butter (diced)

50 g (3) shallots (finely chopped)

2 cloves garlic (finely chopped)

380–400 g (8) Portobello mushrooms (cut into 1 cm thick slices)

240 g (12) button mushrooms (cut into 1 cm thick slices)

120 ml (8 tbsp) port

250 ml (1 cup) cream

20 ml (1 tbsp + 1 tsp) balsamic vinegar

2 tsp wholegrain mustard

1 tsp flaky sea salt

½ tsp freshly ground black pepper

2 tbsp finely chopped chives

4 slices sourdough bread (toasted)

Serve as an autumnal or wintery brunch, light lunch or supper. The ultimate mushrooms to use, of course, would be field mushrooms gathered by you and yours from a paddock close by.

Method

Place a heavy-based frying pan over a medium heat and add half the butter. Once melted, add shallots and cook for 1–2 minutes or till they begin to soften but not to brown.

Add garlic and cook for a further minute or till garlic has softened.

Place second half of butter in pan and melt. Add mushrooms and cook, shaking pan from time to time, till softened and juices are beginning to run.

Pour in port and bring to the boil. Reduce heat and simmer till port and mushroom juices have reduced to around 2 tablespoons.

Add cream, balsamic vinegar, mustard, salt and pepper. Stir constantly for 4–5 minutes till liquids have reduced to a thick creamy sauce.

Season with salt and pepper and sprinkle with chives. Accompany with toasted sourdough and serve immediately.

Braised Beef Short Ribs

Serves 8

105 g (¾ cup) flour

1 tsp flaky sea salt

½ tsp freshly ground black pepper

1.5–1.7 kg (8) boneless beef short ribs (trimmed of excess fat then cut vertically into two)

40 g (4 tbsp) unsalted butter

30 ml (2 tbsp) olive oil

360 g (2 medium) onions (finely diced)

2 cloves garlic (finely chopped)

180 g (1½ med–large) carrots (peeled and diced)

180 g (4 stalks) celery (diced)

2 bay leaves

2 small sprigs rosemary

250 ml (1 cup) red wine

1 litre (4 cups) beef stock (hot)

1 tsp flaky sea salt

½ tsp freshly ground black pepper

This is a great standby winter dish just as braised lamb shanks or Osso Bucco are. Order boneless beef short ribs ahead from the butcher. Best option is to cook ribs the day before and reheat to serve as it gives you the opportunity before reheating to scrape off congealed fat.

Method

Preheat oven to 180 °C.

In a large bowl combine flour, salt and pepper.

Toss short ribs in seasoned flour, shake off excess flour and transfer ribs to a tray.

Melt butter in a heavy-based frying pan over a medium–high heat. Increase temperature to high taking care not to burn the butter. Add short ribs, allowing space in the pan, and seal on all sides till well browned. It may take two to three pan-loads to complete this stage.

Transfer short ribs to a roasting pan sitting ribs snugly together.

Return searing pan to medium heat and add oil and onions. Cook gently for 3–4 minutes or till onions are just soft but not brown.

Add garlic, carrots, celery, bay leaves and rosemary and cook for a further 4–5 minutes or till garlic is soft but not brown and carrot has begun to soften. Spoon over seared ribs.

Return searing pan to a high heat and pour in wine. Bring to the boil, scraping off any browning into the wine, and reduce the wine by half. Add stock with salt and pepper. Bring to the boil then pour into the pan over ribs and vegetables.

Cover roasting dish with aluminium foil and place in oven for 3–3½ hours, or till ribs are very tender and liquids have thickened slightly. If serving immediately cook for 3½ hours. If you intend to cool and reheat later, cook for the lesser time of 3 hours.

Remove from oven and taste for seasoning. Serve immediately or cool and refrigerate to reheat the following day. Accompany with Honeyed Kumara Mash (page 64) and Warm Haricot Beans with Pine Nuts (page 64).

To reheat, remove aluminium foil and scrape fat off surface. Cover once again with aluminium foil and place into 150 °C oven for 1 hour or till heated through.

Honeyed Kumara Mash

Serves 8

850 g (4–6) golden kumara (peeled and chopped into even-sized chunks)

½ tsp flaky sea salt

65 ml (¼ cup) cream (warmed)

40 g (4 tbsp) unsalted butter (diced)

1 tbsp Manuka honey

flaky sea salt

freshly ground black pepper

The sweetness of this mash complements the savouriness of Braised Beef Short Ribs. The mash can be stored for up to two days in the refrigerator, placed into a greased, ovenproof dish, covered with aluminium foil, and reheated in a 150 °C oven for 15–20 minutes.

Method

Place kumara into a medium-size pot and cover with water. Add salt, cover with lid and bring to the boil.

Reduce heat to a simmer and remove lid. Cook for a further 10–15 minutes or till kumara is fork tender.

Drain kumara and, using a potato masher, partly mash the kumara.

Add cream, butter and honey with salt and pepper to taste. Continue to mash till kumara is smooth, then beat with a wooden spoon till creamy and ingredients are combined.

Serve hot.

Warm Haricot Beans with Pine Nuts

Serves 8

145 g dried haricot beans (soaked overnight in cold water and drained) or 400 g drained and rinsed canned beans

45 ml (3 tbsp) extra virgin olive oil

2 tbsp Roasted Garlic (mashed) (see page 162)

50 g (⅓ cup) pine nuts (toasted)

1 tbsp finely chopped Italian parsley leaves

½ tsp finely chopped thyme leaves

½ tsp flaky sea salt

¼ tsp finely ground black pepper

extra virgin olive oil

squeeze of fresh lemon juice

A tasty bean dish is a pleasing textural accompaniment to many winter braised meat dishes.

Method

If using dried beans, place soaked beans into a medium-size pot and cover generously with cold water. Place over a high heat, bring to the boil, reduce heat and cook beans for 2 to 2½ hours or till very tender.

Drain and set aside.

Into the base of a small heavy-based frying pan set over a medium heat pour the oil and heat till hot.

Add beans, garlic and pine nuts, and cook stirring gently for 2–3 minutes till hot and combined.

Remove from heat, and add parsley, thyme, salt and pepper.

Serve hot or warm with an extra drizzle of extra virgin olive oil and squeeze of lemon juice.

Photograph on previous page: Honeyed Kumara Mash (right) and Warm Haricot Beans with Pine Nuts; Braised Beef Shortribs

Spinach and Purslane Salad with Quince Jelly Dressing

Serves 6–8

80 g (3 cups lightly packed) purslane leaves

80 g (4½ cups lightly packed) baby spinach leaves (stalks removed)

60 g (½) red onion (thinly sliced)

20 dried apple slices (purchase or make your own)

50–60 ml Quince Jelly Dressing (see page 159)

Plant salad purslane in your garden and you will be rewarded with this perennial green which tastes like fresh peas. You could, of course, make this salad entirely from spinach.

Method

Place purslane, spinach, half of the red onion slices and half of the dried apple into a large salad bowl.

Drizzle with the Quince Jelly Dressing. Toss well to coat all the leaves.

Sprinkle remaining onion and dried apple over salad and serve immediately.

To make dried apple slices, thinly slice 1 red apple. A mandoline is great for this. Toss in lemon juice. Lay apple slices onto tray of dehydrator and dry overnight till crispy. Store in an airtight container till required.

Leek, Thyme and Feta Galette

Serves 8–10

45 g (3 tbsp) unsalted butter

500 g (5 cups) thinly sliced leeks (white part only)

¼ cup roughly chopped thyme leaves

15 ml (1 tbsp) dry white wine

15 ml (1 tbsp) balsamic vinegar

125 ml (½ cup) sour cream

flaky sea salt and freshly ground pepper

freshly grated nutmeg

1 egg (lightly whisked)

3 tbsp finely chopped Italian parsley leaves

1 recipe Yeast Dough Pastry

220 g feta cheese

¼ cup roughly chopped thyme leaves

1 egg, separated

15 ml (1 tbsp) water

This large open tart is perfect for Sunday lunch. The aroma of yeast dough pastry baking really gets appetites going.

Method

In a heavy-based frying pan set over a low heat melt butter, add leeks and first measure of thyme. Cook over a low heat till leeks are tender.

Increase heat and add wine and balsamic vinegar. Cook till liquids have almost evaporated.

Reduce heat to low, add sour cream, stir in and cook till liquids have reduced by half. Season to taste with salt, pepper and nutmeg.

Remove pan from heat, transfer mixture to a bowl and allow to cool.

Preheat oven to 205 °C. Lightly grease with oil or baking spray a baking tray.

Add first egg and parsley to leek mixture and stir to combine.

Roll out Yeast Dough Pastry on a lightly floured bench to form a 35 cm circle. Transfer dough to prepared tray.

Spread leek filling over dough leaving a 5 cm border.

Cut feta into 5 mm thick slices and arrange over leek filling. Sprinkle second measure thyme onto feta.

Separate second egg and lightly whisk egg white. Fold pastry border over the filling, in a 'pleat-like' fashion, brushing in between the pleats with egg white to make the dough adhere together.

Whisk egg yolk and water together and brush this over the outside of the galette. Place in oven and bake for approximately 20 minutes or till dough is golden and cooked through. Serve warm.

Yeast Dough Pastry	235 g (1 cup + 9½ tbsp) flour
85 ml (⅓ cup) lukewarm water	½ tsp flaky sea salt
1 tsp active dried yeast	1 egg
½ tsp sugar	45 ml (3 tbsp) sour cream

If you wish, make dough the day before, cover and leave in refrigerator overnight. Bring back to room temperature and leave for 1–2 hours till doubled in bulk.

To make Yeast Dough Pastry

Place water, yeast and sugar into a bowl and combine. Cover and leave in a warm room for 10–15 minutes or till it looks foamy.

Add flour, salt, egg and sour cream to yeast mixture and stir till mixture is combined.

Place dough onto a floured bench and knead for 5–10 minutes or till dough is soft, supple and silky.

Place dough in a lightly greased ceramic bowl and cover with plastic wrap. Leave in a warm room for 1–2 hours or till doubled in bulk.

Punch dough down and allow to rest for a few minutes before you roll it out.

Pork Belly in Apple Syrup Marinade

Serves 5–6

1 kg belly pork (skin intact)

125 ml (½ cup) apple syrup (sweet or tart) (available at some supermarkets and specialty food stores)

45 ml (3 tbsp) Tamari sauce (available in Asian section of supermarket)

1½ tsp Szechwan peppers (crushed in a mortar with a pestle or in a spice grinder) (available in Asian section of supermarket)

Succulent roasted pork belly with crispy crackling is a darned good reason for having winter. Seek out New Zealand pork, preferably free range, and always female. Begin this recipe in the morning or, better still, the day before.

Method

Score skin of belly pork on the angle to a depth of 5 mm.

Place belly pork into a large pot, cover with cold water and place a tight-fitting lid on the pot. Bring to the boil and simmer with the lid off for 20–30 minutes, till pork is tender.

Remove pot from heat and, leaving pork in the cooking liquid, completely cool.

Remove pork from cooking liquid. Place into a bowl with apple syrup, Tamari sauce and pepper and combine.

Leave to marinate for 4–6 hours or overnight. Occasionally turn pork around in the marinade.

Preheat oven to 180 °C.

Remove pork from marinade and place onto a roasting tray. For ease of cleaning, line the roasting tray with a Teflon sheet.

Place pork into preheated oven and roast for 30–40 minutes, or till meat is well browned and crackling is crispy.

Remove from oven. To rest pork cover with aluminium foil and sit at room temperature for 15 minutes.

Portion and serve. If you wish, accompany with Spinach and Purslane Salad with Quince Jelly (see page 65).

Sage Chicken with Prosciutto and Vegetables

Serves 8–12, depending
on who wants seconds

15 ml (1 tbsp) olive oil

100 g (12–15 slices)
prosciutto

750 g (3 medium) potatoes

750 g (3 medium) carrots

750 g (4 small) golden
kumara

flaky sea salt and freshly
ground black pepper

2.2 kg (12) corn-fed chicken
thigh (bone in, skin on)

½ cup roughly chopped
fresh sage leaves

350 g (10–12) rindless
bacon rashers

This knockout chicken dish was created by the late Peter Daldin from Otaki, who originated from Italy. Peter served it with a salad of wild rocket leaves dressed with a gutsy extra virgin olive oil.

Method
Preheat oven to 200 °C.

Brush a very large roasting dish with oil. (You could use 2 smaller roasting dishes.)

Lay prosciutto along the bottom of the dish. Peel and roughly chop potatoes, carrots and kumara and lay out over prosciutto. Sprinkle with salt and pepper to taste.

Place chicken thighs, skin side up, on top of vegetables and sprinkle with sage and salt and pepper to taste.

Lay bacon over chicken, then cover the roasting dish with aluminium foil. Place in oven and bake for 15 minutes. Turn heat down to 150 °C and leave to cook for a further 3–3½ hours till chicken and vegetables are meltingly tender.

If you would like to crisp up the bacon and chicken before you serve, place the dish under a hot grill for 5 minutes.

Cover the dish with aluminium foil and sit at room temperature for 10 minutes before serving.

Roasted Winter Vegetable Tarte Tatin

Serves 6–8

340 g (2–3) kumara (peeled and cut into 1.5–2 cm dice)

270g (¼) butternut (peeled and cut into 1.5–2 cm dice)

180 g (1–2) parsnips (peeled and cut into 1.5–2 cm dice)

45 ml (3 tbsp) olive oil

flaky sea salt and freshly ground black pepper

250 g puff pastry

melted butter for greasing tin

½ recipe Caramelised Onions (see page 162) (heated)

A delightful lunch or supper dish served with a salad but this upside-down tart also makes a fine wintery accompaniment to roast beef or lamb.

Method
Preheat oven to 200 °C.

Place kumara onto a low-sided roasting tray, followed by butternut and parsnips. Drizzle vegetables with oil, sprinkle with salt and pepper and toss so that vegetables are coated in oil.

Place into a preheated oven and roast for 8–10 minutes or till vegetables are just tender. Cool.

Roll pastry into a round on a lightly floured work surface to 2 mm thickness. Neaten edges to make a 23 cm round, perhaps using a cake tin base as the template. Rest in refrigerator for 20 minutes.

Increase oven temperature to 220 °C.

Lightly grease with melted butter a 20 cm round, loose-bottom cake tin.

Reheat Caramelised Onions.

Make a single layer of vegetables, packed very tightly together, on the base of tin and top with Caramelised Onions.

Place pastry on top of Caramelised Onions and press edges down the side of tin to cover and surround vegetables.

Place into preheated oven and cook for 15–20 minutes or till pastry is golden.

Remove from oven and cool 2–3 minutes before inverting onto serving plate.

Caramelised Walnut and Apple Tart

Makes one 23 cm tart

1 recipe Sweet Short Pastry

1 egg white (lightly beaten)

120 g (1 cup) walnut halves or pieces (lightly toasted)

Tart Filling (see page 76)

550 g (3) apples (very thinly sliced, a mandoline is great for this) and lightly dressed with juice of 1 lemon

Caramelised Walnuts

Sweet Short Pastry

Makes 1 ball/400 g

200 g (1⅓ cups + 1 tbsp) flour

½ tsp salt

45 g (4½ tbsp) sugar

100 g unsalted butter (cold and finely diced)

1 egg yolk

45 ml (3 tbsp) cold water (approximately)

Caramel, walnut and apple is a flavour combination made in a wintery heaven. Serve with lashings of cream.

Method

Lightly grease with melted butter or baking spray a 23 cm fluted, loose-bottomed tart tin.

Roll pastry on a lightly floured bench into a round, 3 mm in thickness, and approximately 30 cm in diameter.

Line prepared tart tin with the pastry, gently pushing pastry into the base and side. Place in refrigerator for 30 minutes to rest pastry.

Remove pastry-lined tart tin from refrigerator and cover pastry with aluminium foil or baking paper. Fill aluminium foil with raw rice or dried beans.

Preheat oven to 200 °C.

Place pastry-lined tart tin into oven for 7–9 minutes or till sides are three-quarters cooked. Remove aluminium foil and return case to oven for 4–5 minutes or till pastry base is half-cooked. (Keep raw rice or dried beans for next time you bake a pastry base.)

Remove tart base from oven and cool.

Reduce oven temperature to 175 °C.

Lightly brush pastry base with egg white. Sprinkle with toasted walnuts.

Pour in Tart Filling to three-quarters fill pastry shell. You should have a little mixture left over.

Lay out apple slices in concentric circles to completely cover top of filling. Brush apples liberally with remaining filling. Place tart into preheated oven and bake for 20–25 minutes till tart is set but still wobbly in the centre.

Remove tart from oven and decorate top with Caramelised Walnuts.

Return tart to oven for a further 8–10 minutes till walnuts are golden brown and tart is fully set.

Serve warm or at room temperature.

To make Sweet Short Pastry

Into a food processor bowl fitted with a metal blade place flour, salt and sugar.

Caramelised Walnut and Apple Tart – *continued from previous page*

Tart Filling	butter (diced)	Caramelised Walnuts
Makes enough to fill one 23 cm tart	10 g (1½ tbsp) cornflour	Makes 1½ cups
160 ml (⅔ cup less 1 tsp) apple syrup (tart or sweet) (available from some supermarkets and specialty food stores)	15 ml (1 tbsp) water	35 g unsalted butter
	20 ml (1 tbsp plus 1 tsp) brandy	25 ml (1 tbsp + 2 tsp) apple syrup (tart or sweet)
	5 ml (1 tsp) vanilla extract	80 g (6 tbsp + 2 tsp) brown sugar
110 g (½ cup plus 2 tsp) brown sugar	3 eggs	½ tsp vanilla extract
50 g (5 tbsp) unsalted	2 egg yolks	150 g (1½ cups) walnut halves

Sprinkle butter over flour and process till mixture resembles fine breadcrumbs.

In a small jug whisk egg yolk with water.

With food processor running pour egg yolk and water through feed tube. Continue to process till pastry forms a ball and sits above the blade of the machine. If pastry does not form a ball easily, remove mixture from food processor and finish the balling process with your hands.

Knead pastry into a disc-shape, wrap in plastic wrap and rest for 30 minutes in the refrigerator before rolling.

To make Tart Filling
Into a small pot place apple syrup, sugar and butter.

Place over a medium heat and stir till sugar is dissolved. Bring to the boil, reduce heat to a simmer and simmer for 3–4 minutes. Remove pot from heat.

Into a small bowl place cornflour and water and mix to a paste. Add brandy and vanilla and stir well. Slowly pour into apple syrup mixture, whisking at the same time.

Break eggs and yolks into a medium-size bowl and whisk to combine.

Slowly pour eggs into apple syrup mixture, whisking continuously till eggs and apple syrup mixture are combined.

Set mixture aside till ready to use.

To make Caramelised Walnuts
These also make a wonderful garnish on a richly iced chocolate cake but equally they make a sweet, nutty accompaniment to creamy blue cheese.

Place butter, apple syrup and brown sugar into a medium pot and over a gentle heat, stir till sugar is dissolved. Increase heat and boil for 1 minute.

Remove pot from heat and add vanilla and walnut halves. Stir well to coat all walnuts in caramel.

Use within 10 minutes of making otherwise the caramel will firm up and walnuts will clump together.

Kiwifruit, Passionfruit and Mint Salad with Amaretto Dressing

Serves 2–4

280 g (4) kiwifruit (peeled and cut into 5 mm dice)

30 ml (2 tbsp) Passionfruit Syrup (see page 169)

28 g (2 tbsp) ginger in syrup (you find this jarred product in specialty section of supermarket) (cut into 2–3 mm dice)

10 mint leaves (finely sliced)

Amaretto Dressing (see page 169)

A refreshing and simple dessert. Green or gold kiwifruit, or a mixture of both can be used.

Method

In a bowl place kiwifruit, Passionfruit Syrup, ginger and mint.

Stir together and serve in small glasses with Amaretto Dressing.

Baked Gala Apples with Blackcurrants

Serves 8	42 g (8 tsp) brown sugar	1 cinnamon quill
100 g (½ cup) sugar	1 tsp ground cinnamon	185 ml (¾ cup) methode champenoise rosé
finely grated zest of 1 lemon	finely grated zest of 2 lemons	30 ml (2 tbsp) lemon juice
60 g (6 tbsp) unsalted butter (softened)	120 g destalked blackcurrants (fresh or frozen, thawed)	vanilla ice cream and/or whipped cream to serve
1–1.2 kg (8 even-sized) Gala apples (cored with an apple corer and left whole)	1 vanilla bean (sliced in half lengthwise)	

I generally use frozen blackcurrants as they are sold destalked. I always buy New Zealand grown as they are so much plumper and more flavoursome than imported. The idea of baking apples with lemon sugar came from a Martha Stewart recipe and, as Martha suggested, lemon sugar is useful to have in the pantry for sprinkling on cakes and muffins.

Method

To make lemon sugar, in a small bowl place first measure sugar and lemon zest and mix together. Leave for 1–2 hours, or for up to 2–3 weeks, in an airtight jar for flavours to infuse.

Preheat oven to 180 °C.

Using 2 tablespoons butter generously grease base of a large ceramic baking dish and sprinkle with half of the lemon sugar. Trim bases of apples to enable them to sit evenly in the baking dish, and place apples on top of lemon sugar.

In a small bowl combine brown sugar, cinnamon and lemon zest. Evenly fill the centre of each apple with this mixture.

Sprinkle blackcurrants over and around apples, pushing a few into the centre of each.

Spread remaining butter over the top of each apple and sprinkle apples with remaining lemon sugar.

To the baking dish add vanilla bean, cinnamon quill, methode champenoise and lemon juice.

Place in oven and bake for 30–45 minutes or till apples are soft when pierced with a metal skewer.

Serve hot or at room temperature with the syrup and any spilled blackcurrants poured over the top.

If you wish accompany with vanilla ice cream and/or whipped cream.

FOUR

POSH

So the boss is coming to dinner and you need to create a home full of serenity and a show of exceptionally good taste. Make sure you, and the guests, do not have to linger too long over pre-dinner drinks. Too many drinks makes for loose lips, and overcooked food or uncooked food you discover the next day. Streamline your life by pre-setting the table, placing plates in the warming drawer and preparing for the ghastly scenario of a guest saying yes to the offer of coffee. Behave as though you really know what you are doing, and ask guests many questions so that during their answers you can work while you nod, smile and mutter.

Carrot Soup with Scallops and Herb Leaves

Serves 8 as an entrée

375–650 g (24–40) scallops

15 ml (1 tbsp) olive oil

½ tsp flaky sea salt and freshly ground black pepper

¼ cup lightly-packed fresh herb leaves (chervil, coriander, dill, Italian parsley)

Carrot Soup

Carrot Soup

Serves 8 as an entrée

1 litre (4 cups) fresh carrot juice (to make 1 litre of fresh carrot juice you will need 4–4.5 kg of fresh carrots)

500 ml (2 cups) sauvignon blanc

185 ml (¾ cup) lemon juice

180 g (1⅓ cups) finely chopped shallots

1 tsp flaky sea salt

4 tsp finely grated fresh ginger

This entrée is as light and fresh as air. Whispers of scallops and herb flavours with sweet-tasting soup.

Method
Preheat oven to 220 °C.

Place scallops on a low-sided baking tray, drizzle with oil and sprinkle with salt and pepper. Toss ingredients together so scallops are coated in oil. Spread scallops out onto tray so they do not touch.

Place scallops into oven and hot roast for 4–5 minutes or till scallops become opaque. Flesh should still feel soft to the touch.

Into 8 wide-based warmed soup bowls place scallops and a generous sprinkle of herbs.

Pour 150 ml (½ cup + 2½ tbsp) Carrot Soup into each bowl and serve.

Freshly made carrot juice, available at juice bars, has a very short refrigerator life, so buy and freeze till you are ready to make this soup. Alternatively buy a vegetable juicer and juice carrots yourself.

To make Carrot Soup
Pour carrot juice, sauvignon blanc and lemon juice into a large, wide-based pot.

Add shallots and salt. Place over a medium-high heat and bring to a boil.

Add ginger and simmer rapidly till liquid has reduced by half.

Strain and discard all solids. Season with extra salt and pepper if necessary and reheat to serve.

Salmon Wrapped in Nori with Lime Wasabi Dressing

Serves 8–9 as an entrée or 4–5 as a main course

900 g–1 kg salmon fillet (skin off and pin boned)

3–4 nori sheets

Cucumber and Radish Salad

Lime Wasabi Dressing (see page 159)

kelp pepper for sprinkling

Pink, black, soft green, red and white is the palette of this impressive-looking dish. Accompany with wilted spinach with sesame seeds or green beans with Lemon Infused Olive Oil (page 168). Kelp pepper is available at specialty food stores.

Method

Trim belly edge of salmon fillet about 1 cm in from the edge as this thin edge tends to overcook. Retain belly edge for another use. Lay salmon, skin side facing you (but skin has been removed), on a clean work surface.

Cut one of the nori sheets into two 5 cm wide strips. Lay these strips lengthwise down the centre of the salmon. Trim strips to the same length as salmon fillet.

Starting from the belly edge tightly roll salmon to enclose nori.

On a clean work surface spread out a large piece of plastic wrap 10 cm longer than length of salmon fillet.

Place the 2 remaining nori sheets, slightly overlapping, on the plastic wrap. Position the rolled salmon 2–3 cm in from the nori edge closest to you. If the salmon is too long for the nori, add another sheet. Lightly brush the top and bottom edges of the nori with water.

Using plastic wrap as a guide, tightly wrap salmon completely in nori. If you have a gap, cover it with a strip of nori. Roll completely in plastic wrap and rest in refrigerator 1–2 hours.

Preheat oven to 180 °C.

Remove salmon from plastic wrap and place on a low-sided baking tray preferably lined with a Teflon sheet or alternatively lightly greased with olive oil.

Place in oven and bake for 15–18 minutes or till just cooked. Salmon will be overcooked if milky juices begin to exude.

Remove from oven and rest under a tea towel for 5–10 minutes before serving.

Cucumber and Radish Salad	20 g (2) radishes (washed, trimmed and julienned)
Serves 8	16–20 small mint leaves
100 g (½) cucumber (peeled, seeded and julienned)	24–28 small coriander leaves

Using a sharp knife portion into slices and place portions in the centre of warmed, large dinner plates.

Pile Cucumber and Radish Salad on top of each and drizzle Lime Wasabi Dressing over and around salmon. Sprinkle with kelp pepper and serve immediately.

To make Cucumber and Radish Salad
In a medium-size bowl toss together cucumber, radish, mint and coriander.

Cover and refrigerate till ready to use.

Julienne refers to little matchsticks. Julienned raw vegetables can be crisscrossed or can stand up on a plate. Cucumber and radish can be prepared a day ahead and placed on wet paper towels in a covered container in the refrigerator.

West Coast Whitebait with Zucchini Ribbons

Serves 6 as an entrée

600–700g (6 small) zucchini (ends removed)

45 ml (3 tbsp) freshly squeezed lemon juice

45 ml (3 tbsp) extra virgin olive oil

30 ml (2 tbsp) Lemon Infused Olive Oil (see page 168)

360 g West Coast whitebait (drained in a sieve and placed onto paper towels)

freshly ground white pepper and flaky sea salt

extra Lemon Infused Olive Oil for drizzling

West Coast whitebait is New Zealand's best kept secret. Fritters made with the little fish are iconic but lift the bar, go all out and serve whitebait out of a batter.

Method

Slice zucchini into very long, thin ribbons. A mandoline or a Rex peeler will make this a simple job. Discard the first and last ribbons, which are mainly skin.

Place zucchini ribbons into a small bowl and add lemon juice and extra virgin olive oil. Toss with your hands to combine and leave to macerate for 2–3 hours at room temperature. Do not toss with a metal fork as this will bruise the ribbons.

Pour 2 tablespoons Lemon Infused Olive Oil into a small, heavy-based frying pan and place over a medium heat. When hot scatter whitebait into frying pan, but do not crowd the pan, and cook on one side for 30 seconds only.

Holding the handle of the frying pan, and using a slice or metal scraper, very quickly turn whitebait over. Cook for a further 30 seconds or till whitebait has changed from translucent to opaque. To prevent whitebait cooking further quickly remove whitebait to a warmed ceramic dish.

To serve, into the centre of each warmed serving plate pile 4–6 zucchini ribbons and top with equal amounts of whitebait. Season to taste.

Drizzle the plate with a little extra Lemon Infused Olive Oil.

Corn-fed Chicken with Vegetables and Tarragon Sauce

Serves 4–6

1 size 14 corn-fed chicken

370 g (2) onions (each cut into 6 wedges)

1 tsp flaky sea salt

½ tsp freshly ground black pepper

2 sprigs thyme

2 bay leaves

200 g (1½ –2) carrots (peeled and cut into batons)

230 g (1½ –2) parsnips (peeled and cut into batons)

660 g (3–4) Agria potatoes (peeled and cut into large wedges)

Tarragon Sauce

The smell of slowly simmering chicken with vegetables will make guests' mouths water. Do as the best airlines do and serve comfort food to your first class passengers.

Method

Rinse chicken in cold running water and pat dry with paper towels. Fold each wing back on itself to hold wings in place.

Place chicken into a large casserole or heavy-based pot which will tolerate direct heat. I like to use a Le Creuset cast-iron casserole I have owned for years.

Add onions, salt, pepper, thyme and bay leaves. Add cold water to casserole to cover chicken. Place lid on casserole and place casserole on stove top over a medium heat. Cook for around 15 minutes or till water comes to the boil. Reduce heat to low, and cook for a further 30 minutes with lid slightly ajar.

Add carrots, parsnips and potatoes to casserole. Place lid back on casserole, slightly ajar. Increase heat and bring back to the boil, then reduce to a low heat and simmer for a further 25–35 minutes, or till chicken juices run clear. Test chicken by inserting a metal skewer into the chicken where the thigh is attached to the body.

Remove chicken and vegetables to a warm platter and cover with aluminium foil. Rest away from heat for up to 20 minutes. Strain cooking liquid, reserving to make Tarragon Sauce to serve with the chicken and hoping there will be enough cooking liquid, leftover chicken and vegetables to make chicken soup the following day.

Portion chicken, accompany with vegetables, and serve with Tarragon Sauce.

Photograph on opposite page: Corn-fed Chicken with Vegetables and Tarragon Sauce

Tarragon Sauce

Makes 300ml

30 g (3 tbsp) unsalted butter

21 g (3 tbsp) flour

190 ml (1¾ cups) chicken cooking liquid

85 ml (⅓ cup) cream

2 tbsp roughly chopped tarragon leaves

1 tbsp finely sliced chives

1 tbsp roughly cut Italian parsley leaves

flaky sea salt and freshly ground black pepper

freshly ground nutmeg

French tarragon is a perennial and thrives in our garden right through summer. We freeze surplus to use in dishes such as this.

To make Tarragon Sauce

Into a medium-sized pot set over a low heat place butter and melt. Add flour and stir well to combine. Cook butter and flour for 3–4 minutes or till mixture begins to smell nutty.

Slowly add chicken cooking liquid stirring well between additions till all the liquid is incorporated and the sauce is smooth and thick. Continue to cook on a very low heat for 5 minutes or till sauce has a silky finish.

Stir in cream, tarragon, chives and parsley, and season to taste with salt, pepper and nutmeg. Serve immediately, or slowly reheat to serve at a later stage.

Frenched Lamb Racks with Lemon and Peppercorn Paste and Spring Herb Dressing

Serves 6

5 tsp finely grated lemon zest

1½ tsp pink peppercorns (in brine, rinsed)

1½ tsp green peppercorns (in brine, rinsed)

1½ tsp muscovado sugar

1 tbsp finely chopped dill

900 g–1.1 kg (3) Frenched lamb racks (8 cutlets per rack)

30 ml (2 tbsp) olive oil

Spring Herb Dressing (see page 166)

A small amount of well-flavoured paste produces an incredibly zesty flavour. Accompany lamb with Buttered Herbed Potatoes (see page 123) and peas cooked with mint.

Method

Into a mortar place lemon zest, pink and green peppercorns and sugar. Using a pestle pound to a paste. Stir in dill.

Rub paste all over the lamb racks and massage the racks with the paste. Marinate lamb in refrigerator for a minimum of 4 hours or overnight.

Preheat oven to 200 °C.

Place a small roasting dish into the oven for 5 minutes or till it is very hot.

Smear pan with oil, place lamb in pan and then into oven. Roast for 8 minutes, turn lamb over, and cook for a further 8–9 minutes or till lamb is cooked medium–rare.

Remove from oven and rest at room temperature for 10 minutes covered with a clean, heavy tea towel.

Portion lamb racks into double cutlets, serving 2 double cutlets per guest with Spring Herb Dressing.

Roast Fillet of Beef, Herbed Eggplant and Salsa Verde

Serves 8

30 ml (2 tbsp) olive oil

1 or 2 sprigs thyme, sage or rosemary

1.5–1.8 kg beef fillet (trimmed of silverskin)

freshly ground black pepper

Herbed Eggplant

Salsa Verde (see page 153)

Herbed Eggplant

Serves 8

85 ml (⅓ cup) olive oil

700 g (4) small eggplants (cut lengthwise into 1.5 cm thick slices)

30 ml (2 tbsp) balsamic vinegar

45 ml (3 tbsp) extra virgin olive oil

3 tbsp sliced basil

1 tbsp chopped chives

1 tbsp finely chopped Italian parsley leaves

flaky sea salt and freshly ground black pepper

Roasting a whole fillet of beef and serving with interesting accompaniments is the simple answer to impressive entertaining.

Method

Preheat oven to 220 °C.

Lightly grease a low-sided roasting tray with oil and place thyme, sage or rosemary sprigs on tray.

Brush oil over beef and season with pepper. Place beef in oven and roast for 20 minutes or till cooked medium–rare.

To rest beef cover tray with a heavy tea towel and sit at room temperature for 10–15 minutes.

Portion beef to present on individual plates or on a platter and serve with Herbed Eggplant and Salsa Verde.

Take the fillet out of the refrigerator 30–60 minutes before roasting it.

To make Herbed Eggplant

Preheat barbecue, or a grill plate set over stove top, to high.

Pour first measure of oil over eggplant slices and mix to coat all slices.

Lay eggplant slices on barbecue or grill plate and cook for 4–5 minutes on each side, or till dark golden and fork-tender. If it suits you, begin on barbecue then remove eggplant to a low-sided baking tray and place in 160 °C oven till eggplant is fork-tender.

Combine eggplant, balsamic vinegar, second measure of oil, basil, chives, parsley and salt and pepper in a large bowl and serve immediately or chill to serve later. Remove from refrigerator 30 minutes before serving.

Golden Kiwifruit Crème Brûlée

Serves 8

8 golden kiwifruit

300 ml (1 cup + 3 tbsp + 1 tsp) cream

½ vanilla pod (cut in half lengthwise)

3 egg yolks

15g (1½ tbsp) sugar

extra sugar for brûléeing

This is a crème brûlée formed and served in a scooped-out golden kiwifruit. It takes on a tropical flavour and was first prepared for me by Chef Stephen Barry from Tauranga and I loved it.

Method

Slice top off each kiwifruit like you would the top off a boiled egg and, using a teaspoon, scoop out the centre of each to form a case, but leave a 5 mm–1 cm wall of flesh in the case. Reserve scooped-out fruit for another use such as fruit salad or smoothies. Ever so slightly trim the bottom of the kiwifruit so it sits flat on a plate but doesn't form an opening.

In a heavy-bottomed saucepan, set over a medium heat, pour cream, add vanilla and bring to the boil. Take off heat and let sit for at least 60 seconds.

Place egg yolks in a bowl and whisk till just combined. Add sugar and whisk till pale and frothy. Add hot cream to yolks, mixing well but not whisking. Strain mixture back into a clean saucepan and return to a low heat, stirring continuously with a wooden spoon till mixture thickens enough to cover the back of the wooden spoon. Remove from heat and allow to cool slightly.

Pour custard into a jug and fill hollowed-out kiwifruit cases with custard right up to the top. Chill for 4 hours or overnight.

Just before serving sprinkle custard surface with a little sugar and, using a chef's torch, brûlée sugar till it is golden brown and caramelised.

If you wish accompany with Kiwifruit, Passionfruit and Mint Salad (see page 77).

Pear, Banana and Date Tart

Makes one 35 cm x 10 cm tart or serves 8			Sweet Pastry
200 g (1.5) ripe pears (peeled, halved and cored)	160 g (8) Medjool dates (halved and pitted)	15 ml (1 tbsp) rum	140 g (1 cup) flour
115 g (1) banana (peeled)	150 g (½ cup + 3 tbsp + 2 tsp) mascarpone	seeds from vanilla pod (or ½ tsp vanilla extract)	85 g (¼ cup plus 4 tbsp) caster sugar
20 g (2 tbsp) unsalted butter	40 g (4 tbsp) sugar	35 cm x 10 cm sweet pastry case (blind baked)	75 g unsalted butter (cold and diced)
	2 eggs (lightly whisked)	48 g (4 tbsp) brown sugar	30–45 ml (2–3 tbsp) water

We make this tart in a rectangular loose-bottomed tin as it allows for even cooking and easy portioning. Fresh dates are available in the produce section of your supermarket and I always look for Medjools.

Method
Preheat oven to 170 °C.

Slice each pear half into 4–5 slices (2.5–3 cm thick wedges).

Cut banana in half lengthwise and then each half into 3 widthwise.

In a small, heavy-based frying pan over a low heat place butter and melt. Add pears and dates and cook for 3–4 minutes till pears are just beginning to soften. Add banana and cook a further 1 minute or till banana is slightly browned on the outside.

Remove from heat and tip into a bowl to cool quickly.

In a medium-size bowl place mascarpone, sugar, eggs, rum and vanilla seeds or vanilla extract and whisk to combine.

Evenly scatter fruit, ensuring uncut side of date is facing you, over the base of the pastry case and pour mascarpone mixture into pastry case.

Sprinkle with half the brown sugar and bake in preheated oven 20–25 minutes till just set. Serve warm rather than hot, and when you are ready to serve sprinkle remaining brown sugar over tart and place under a hot grill for 30–60 seconds or till the brown sugar just begins to melt.

If you wish, serve with whipped cream flavoured with vanilla paste or extract and sweetened with sugar.

Sweet Pastry Method
In the bowl of a food processor fitted with a metal blade place flour, sugar and butter. Process till mixture resembles coarse breadcrumbs.

With processor running slowly pour in 2 tablespoons water. Add remaining 1 tablespoon water if the mixture isn't coming together easily. Process till pastry just begins to form a ball.

Banana and Date Tart – *continued from previous page*

Tip onto a lightly floured bench and knead for 1 minute to form a smooth ball. Flatten out to a disc-shape, wrap in plastic wrap and refrigerate to rest 30 minutes before using.

To bake blind

Grease tin with baking spray or melted butter.

Roll pastry into a rectangular shape about 45 cm x 20 cm (for a rectangular tin 35 cm x 10 cm) and to a 3 mm thickness. Retain any leftover pastry for patching.

Place pastry into greased tart tin gently pushing pastry into base and sides. Leave pastry 2–3 mm above the edge of the tart tin.

Cover pastry with aluminium foil or baking paper and fill aluminium foil-lined pastry case with raw rice or dried beans.

Place tart shell in refrigerator for 30 minutes to rest pastry.

Preheat oven to 200 ºC.

Place tart shell into oven for 10–12 minutes or till pastry is just starting to colour.

Remove aluminium foil. Trim pastry overhang with a sharp knife. If there are holes or cracks in the pastry case patch up with leftover pastry. Return pastry case to oven for a further 5–7 minutes or till pastry is light golden and cooked through (reserve baking rice or beans for the next time you blind bake).

Remove from oven and cool.

Fudgy Chocolate and Ginger Mousse

Serves 6–8

140 g dark (70%) chocolate (tablet cut into small pieces)

15 ml (1 tbsp) water

4 eggs (separated)

70 g (⅓ cup) caster sugar

25 g (1½ knobs) ginger in syrup (drained and cut into fine dice)

Chocolate and ginger is a dynamic combination in this incredibly fudgy and rich mousse. Plan on serving small portions, ideally served with Baked Pears in Verjuice with Vanilla (see page 101).

Method

Place chocolate and water into a heatproof bowl and place bowl over a small pot of simmering water. The bowl needs to fit snugly into the pot. Stir chocolate and water till chocolate just begins to melt. Remove bowl from pot and stir to combine with water off the heat.

Cool chocolate for a few moments.

Place egg yolks in a separate bowl and whisk till combined well. Add chocolate and whisk to combine. Return bowl to sit over pot of simmering water and stir with a wooden spoon till mixture just thickens. When you run a finger down the back of the spoon to create a line and the line remains, the mixture is thick enough.

In a clean bowl place egg whites and whisk till fluffy. Gradually pour in sugar, whisking continuously till a meringue consistency is reached.

Fold egg white mixture and ginger into chocolate mixture, being careful not to deflate egg whites. Portion into dessert glasses, or a bowl to scoop or spoon mousse from, and refrigerate for a minimum of 3 hours or up to 2 days.

Photograph on following page: Fudgy Chocolate and Ginger Mousse with Baked Pears in Verjuice with Vanilla

Baked Pears in Verjuice with Vanilla

Serves 6–8

400 g (2 cups) sugar

335 ml (1⅓ cups) water

750 g (4) ripe pears
(peeled, halved and core
scooped out)

335 ml (1⅓ cups) verjuice

1½ vanilla beans (halved
lengthwise)

Sweet luscious pears baked with acidity are the perfect foil for Fudgy Chocolate and Ginger Mousse. Use a melon baller to scoop out pear core neatly.

Method
Preheat oven to 180 °C.

In a small pot place sugar and water and place over a low heat. Stir till sugar is dissolved. Bring to the boil and remove from heat.

Cut a very thin slice off the rounded side of each pear half so each pear half sits level.

Place pears cut-side down in a medium-size ceramic dish and add hot syrup, verjuice and then add vanilla beans. Place a cartouche on top of pears (this is a piece of greaseproof paper cut to fit the dish, which weights the pears down so they stay submerged in the liquid).

Place dish in oven and bake pears for 20–30 minutes or till fork-tender. Less ripe pears may take 40–60 minutes. Remove dish from oven.

Carefully drain three-quarters of the syrup from the baking dish into a small pot. Place pot over a medium heat and bring to the boil. Simmer for 7–8 minutes to reduce syrup and improve colour.

Serve pears warm or cold surrounded by poaching syrup. Store for up to 3 days in refrigerator. Leftover syrup can be stored, chilled, to use again.

Manuka Honey Ice Cream with Chilli-spiced Almonds with Cumin

Serves 5–6

120 g (⅓ cup) Manuka honey

4 egg yolks

300 ml cream (lightly whipped)

120 g Chilli-spiced Almonds with Cumin (see page 21)

Technically speaking this ice-cream recipe is a frozen parfait as opposed to ice cream. It has a higher ratio of fat than an ice-cream mixture, which is generally egg yolks and milk or milk and cream, as this recipe uses egg yolks and cream only. An ice-cream churn is not required to break up the ice crystals as it freezes and it will be softer than ice cream.

Method

Place honey into a small, heavy-bottomed saucepan and slowly bring to the boil while stirring with a metal spoon. Allow the honey to boil for 2 minutes.

Place egg yolks into a bowl and begin to whisk, and as you whisk, slowly pour hot honey into egg yolks, and then whisk at high speed till the mixture has cooled, is whitish in colour and has doubled in volume.

Fold cream into egg yolk mixture being careful to maintain the volume of the egg yolk mixture. Pour mixture into a plastic bowl or container, cover and freeze overnight. Store in freezer tightly covered overnight or for up to 1 week.

To serve, coarsely chop Chilli-spiced Almonds with Cumin. Scoop ice cream into serving dishes and sprinkle with the chopped nuts.

FIVE

CELEBRATIONS

Celebrate beginnings, middles and ends of seasons, New Year, Valentine's Day, end of school year, Christmas, birthdays, anniversaries, Easter, end of the week, Saturdays and Sundays. There are so many occasions to celebrate. You can have a celebration every day if you are up to it. People who love good food embrace life and will find this a reason, as much as designated days, for festivity. Sharing food at a table is also sharing *joie de vivre*, bonhomie and spirituality. Raise a glass to celebrate life and be thankful that you have been given an entitlement to bountiful food.

Crayfish and Avocado Salad with David's Tangy Lemon Dressing

Serves 8

4 cooked and prepared crayfish tails

8 handfuls salad greens (the smaller the leaves, the better)

4 avocados (halved, stone removed and thickly sliced)

3 oranges (peeled and segmented)

David's Tangy Lemon Dressing (see page 156)

The tried and true combination of crayfish, avocado and citrus is a match made in heaven. This is a dreamlike way of beginning a celebration meal.

Method
Halve crayfish tail flesh lengthwise.

Place a handful of salad greens into centre of each serving plate or on a platter and arrange crayfish, avocado, and orange segments amongst salad greens.

Drizzle salad generously with David's Tangy Lemon Dressing and serve immediately.

To cook and prepare crayfish tails
Take 4 (1.6 kg–2 kg total weight) small live crayfish and 1 teaspoon flaky sea salt.

Firstly drown crayfish by plunging into a large sink of cold water and leaving for up to 20 minutes or till they stop kicking. Bring a large pot of water to the boil and add salt.

Place crayfish in boiling water and cook for 5–6 minutes (allow 12 minutes per kg weight) or till crayfish have turned deep red. Gently drain into a large colander. Once cool, twist and pull crayfish tails from bodies. Reserve bodies for another use. Using kitchen scissors cut up both sides of the underside of crayfish tails. Remove underside and loosen flesh from tails. Serve immediately or refrigerate for up to 1 day.

Celebration Seafood Salad

(Serves 10)

1 whole 1–1.5 kg fish

450 g (20) prawns (peeled with tails intact)

300 g (20) scallops

30 ml (2 tbsp) olive oil

flaky sea salt and freshly ground black pepper

110–130 g (20) French beans (tops removed)

290–300 g (20) baby carrots (scraped)

340–380 g (20) cauliflower florets

190 g (1) red capsicum (deseeded and sliced)

90–110g (20) snow peas (topped and tailed)

20 live mussels (washed and beards removed)

150 g (5) generous handfuls of rocket leaves (or other small and soft salad greens)

30 Crostini

Herbed Caper Sauce (see page 155)

1 kg graded small new potatoes (simmered till fork tender)

20 Pacific oysters (in the half shell)

Twenty years ago our first-ever cooking class was taken by Audris d'Aragona and Alice Pugh who operated a restaurant and The Roman Cooking School just outside of Rome. This monumental dish from their class has remained a part of my repertoire ever since and is the perfect all-in-one seafood dish for a celebration.

Method

Preheat oven to 250 °C. Brush fish with olive oil and place on a low-sided baking tray. Bake for 15 minutes or till a metal skewer easily pierces flesh. Cool, remove skin and discard. Flake fish.

Toss prawns and scallops in olive oil, sprinkle with salt and pepper and spread onto a low-sided baking tray. Place in oven for 5 minutes or till prawns turn pink and scallops become opaque.

Bring a large pot of water to boil and plunge beans, carrots, cauliflower, red capsicum and snow peas into water. When water returns to the boil remove vegetables and plunge into icy water. Drain and dry.

Pour water into a medium-size pot to come 2.5 cm up sides and place mussels into water.

Cover, place on a medium heat and steam mussels for 10–15 minutes or till they open. Remove and cool.

To assemble, line a large platter with rocket. Spread Crostini with Herbed Caper Sauce and arrange Crostini in a single layer on rocket.

Slice potatoes into fat discs and spread Herbed Caper Sauce onto one side of potatoes. Lay potato discs onto Crostini.

Onto potato discs place some fish and lay some vegetables onto fish.

Repeat layers, building a pyramid shape and finishing with potatoes. Garnish outside of the pyramid with prawns, scallops and oysters.

Accompany with any remaining Crostini and Herbed Caper Sauce.

To make Crostini

Preheat oven to 150 °C. Slice 1 French stick into 1 cm slices and brush each side lightly with olive oil. Place on a baking tray and then into oven. Bake for 25–30 minutes or till bread is light golden brown. Store in an airtight container till ready to use or for up to 3 days.

Whole Roast Turkey with Old-fashioned Herb Stuffing, Trivet Potatoes and Pan Gravy

Serves 10–12

500 g unsalted butter (melted) (don't panic, you may not require all of this!)

2 kg potatoes (with skin on) (Agria would be a good choice)

flaky sea salt and freshly ground black pepper

1 x 5–6 kg turkey

Old-fashioned Herb Stuffing

500 g rindless bacon rashers

1 piece muslin (50 cm long x 90 cm wide)

190 ml (¾ cup) dry white wine

315 ml (1¼ cups) chicken stock

Pan Gravy

Old-fashioned Herb Stuffing

Makes enough to stuff a 5–6 kg turkey

60 g (6 tbsp) unsalted butter

180 g (1 large) onion (peeled and finely chopped)

This may not be enough potatoes for your hungry mob on Christmas day. If so, slice extra potatoes and place in a greased roasting tray, single layer, and cover with additional chicken stock and white wine. Bake for approximately 2 hours in the oven containing the turkey or till cooking liquid is absorbed and potatoes are golden brown.

Method

Preheat oven to 210 ºC. Grease base of a large deep-sided roasting tray with a little butter. Cut potatoes into 1.5–2 cm thick slices and lay slices, not overlapping, in the base of the roasting tray. Brush with a little butter and season with salt and pepper.

Remove offal from turkey and reserve for Pan Gravy. Wash turkey inside and out and pat dry. Season inside with salt and pepper.

Fill turkey's cavity with Old-Fashioned Herb Stuffing. Tie the legs together tightly with string and place turkey onto potatoes. Brush the turkey with a little butter and season with salt and pepper. Lay the rashers of bacon over the turkey, particularly the breast of the bird.

Place muslin into butter, remove, and drape over turkey to cover completely. Pour white wine and chicken stock around turkey, place in oven and roast for 30 minutes. Baste turkey (i.e. baste buttered muslin) with juices in pan and a little more butter.

Reduce oven temperature to 180 °C. Bake for a further 3–3½ hours or till turkey juices run clear, basting every 30 minutes with juices in pan and a little more butter.

When cooked, remove turkey from oven and place turkey on a platter. Cover turkey in aluminium foil and rest for 20–30 minutes.

Drain fat and juices from roasting tray and reserve for a later use. Cover potatoes with aluminium foil and return tray to warming drawer to keep potatoes crisp and warm.

To serve, remove stuffing from turkey and slice. Portion turkey into body parts and slice each body part, e.g. remove a breast and slice the breast. Place onto platter or serving plates with potatoes. Accompany with Pan Gravy and green vegetables of your choice – minted green peas work really well.

100 g (6–7) shallots (peeled and finely chopped)

450 g fresh breadcrumbs (day-old white bread crumbed in food processor)

2 tbsp finely chopped sage leaves

2 tbsp finely chopped thyme leaves

3 eggs

flaky sea salt and freshly ground pepper

Pan Gravy

Serves 10–12

1 tbsp olive oil

turkey offal to include neck, giblets, heart and liver

250 g (2 medium) onions (peeled and sliced)

250 g (2 large) carrots (peeled and sliced)

2 cloves garlic (peeled)

125 ml (½ cup) white wine

bay leaf + 3 stalks thyme (tied together with culinary string)

1.25 litres (5 cups) chicken stock liquid (hot)

40 g (4 tbsp) butter

42 g (6 tbsp) flour

flaky sea salt and freshly ground black pepper

Onion and shallot softened in butter, fresh breadcrumbs with a generous amount of fresh herbs make this stuffing taste like a herb stuffing should.

To make Old-fashioned Herb Stuffing

Place butter into a small frying pan set over a medium heat and melt. Add onion and shallots and cook till transparent but not browned. Cool.

Place onion mixture in a bowl with breadcrumbs, sage, thyme and eggs. Mix together and season to taste.

To make Pan Gravy

To make stock for gravy, preheat oven to 180 °C. Brush an ovenproof frying pan with olive oil and add turkey neck, giblets, onions, carrots and garlic. Retain heart and liver. Place frying pan in oven and roast for 45–55 minutes or till neck and vegetables are well browned.

Transfer contents of pan to a medium-size pot. Place frying pan onto medium heat. Pour wine into frying pan, add bay leaf and thyme and reduce liquid to a quarter of the original volume. Pour onto ingredients in pot and add turkey heart, liver and chicken stock. Simmer till volume has reduced by half. Strain stock.

Over a medium heat, melt butter in a pot and once hot, add flour. Cook for 4–5 minutes, stirring occasionally till roux changes to a fawn colour and smells nutty.

Gradually add hot stock, whisking constantly to prevent lumps from forming. Bring to the boil and simmer for 15–20 minutes to cook out flour. If made on the day, add any turkey juices produced during resting and season to taste.

If time permits remove offal from turkey ahead of preparing turkey so it is possible to prepare the gravy ahead. If this isn't an option but you do wish to prepare ahead then substitute turkey offal with chicken offal. If made ahead chill for up to 3 days or freeze for up to 2 weeks.

Photograph on following page: Whole Roast Turkey with Old-Fashioned Herb Stuffing, Trivet Potatoes and Pan Gravy

Standing Rib Roast of Beef with Caperberry Vinaigrette

Serves 8–10

2.5 kg standing rib roast of beef (ask butcher to tie it with string)

freshly ground black pepper

Caperberry Vinaigrette (see page 153)

Beetroot and Horseradish Condiment (see page 165)

There's nothing quite like a well-aged piece of beef roasted on the bone.

Method
Preheat oven to 200 °C.

Place a dry roasting pan on a high heat and when pan is hot add beef and sear on all sides till well browned.

Temporarily remove beef from pan and set a rack in base of roasting pan. Place beef onto rack and sprinkle generously with pepper. Place into preheated oven and roast for 1 hour 20 minutes or till internal temperature is 55 °C or just below medium–rare.

Remove beef from oven.

To rest: Cover with several tea towels, tucking tea towels under base of the tray rather than in the tray and sit beef at room temperature for 30 minutes. This will take the internal temperature to 60 °C or medium–rare, distribute juices throughout the meat and make carving a more streamlined process.

Transfer beef to chopping board and remove string. Using a fork to hold beef in place, cut down and along rib bones to remove beef in one piece. Set beef, cut-side down, and carve across the grain into 10–16 slices.

Serve hot with Caperberry Vinaigrette and Beetroot and Horseradish Condiment. Offer the bones when you offer second helpings!

For perfectly cooked meat take the guesswork out by testing for temperature with a digital meat probe which is available at kitchen shops. An internal temperature of 60 °C indicates medium–rare beef, so remove beef from oven when the internal temperature reads 55 °C and during the resting time the temperature will increase to 60 °C. For medium beef remove beef at 60 °C internal temperature and rest for 30 minutes which will take the internal temperature to 65 °C.

Roasted Garlic Yorkshire Puddings

Makes 18 baby Yorkshire puddings

105 g (¾ cup) flour

pinch salt

2 eggs (lightly beaten)

250 ml (1 cup) milk

2 cloves garlic crushed with ½ tsp salt

Duck Fat or clarified butter

18 whole cloves Roasted Garlic (see page 162)

Roasted Garlic Yorkshire Puddings add the final touch to tasty roast beef. Potatoes roasted in duck fat moves roasted potatoes up several notches and the same is true with Yorkshire puddings.

Method

Sieve flour and salt into a medium-size bowl. Add eggs, milk, crushed garlic and whisk till smooth.

Rest batter in the refrigerator for 1 hour or overnight.

Preheat oven to 220 ºC.

Grease a 12-cup and a 6-cup baby muffin tray with baking spray or oil and into each place ¼ tsp Duck Fat or clarified butter.

Place muffin trays into oven and heat for 3–5 minutes or till fat or butter is sizzling.

Whisk mixture well and pour into muffin tins till 2–3 mm from the top.

Drop 1 roasted garlic clove into centre of each pudding.

Bake for 20–25 minutes till double in size and a rich golden brown. Tip out onto a cooling rack and eat as soon as possible.

To render Duck Fat

Heat oven to 150 ºC. Place duck skin with fat attached, or fat taken from duck, into ovenproof dish with lid on. Place into preheated oven and cook for 1 hour, stirring once or twice during the cooking time. Remove from oven and drain fat through a sieve into a bowl. Store fat in refrigerator or freeze till required.

Parsnips and Shallots with Macadamia Nuts

Serves 6–8

250 g (8–10) shallots

2 tsp grapeseed oil

½ tbsp butter

615 g (4 small) parsnips (peeled and cut into 2 cm-thick slices, cut on a severe angle)

flaky sea salt and freshly ground black pepper

100 ml (⅓ cup + 1 tbsp) chicken stock liquid

100 g raw whole macadamias

½ tsp finely chopped thyme leaves

This is a hearty accompaniment to Standing Rib Roast of Beef (see page 114) but as a dish in its own right it will be particularly enjoyed by non-meat-eating guests.

Method

Place shallots with skin on into pot of boiling water. Bring water back to the boil and boil for 4 minutes. Drain into a sieve and rinse shallots under cold running water for 1 minute. Trim root end of each shallot and peel.

Preheat oven to 190 °C.

Place oil and butter into a low-sided baking tray and place into oven for 2–3 minutes or till hot. Add parsnips and shallots, toss well and sprinkle with salt and pepper.

Return to oven and cook vegetables for 25–30 minutes or till golden brown and soft.

Place chicken stock, macadamias and thyme into a small pot and place over a medium heat. Bring to a simmer and simmer till liquids have reduced by half. Season to taste with salt and pepper.

Remove roasted parsnips and shallots from oven, pour macadamia mixture into tray and toss together. Season if necessary and serve hot.

Double Lamb Forequarter with Roasted Vegetable Stuffing and Beetroot Jus

Serves 15–20

30 ml (2 tbsp) olive oil

1 x 7 kg double lamb forequarter (with rib bones and shanks removed but back bone remaining)

Roasted Vegetable Stuffing

625 ml (2½ cups) sauvignon blanc

culinary string

Beetroot Jus (see page 161) (heated)

continued over page—

To make this feasting dish visit your butcher ahead so the cut can be prepared for you. The forequarter is the sweetest part of a lamb. In our recipe it includes 10 ribs per side. If you decrease to 7 ribs this will decrease the per/kg price as your butcher will not be cutting into the lamb cutlets which he sells as Frenched lamb rack. Our double forequarter comes from a 17 kg lamb.

Method

Preheat oven to 200 °C. Lightly grease a very large roasting tray with oil.

Place double lamb forequarter onto a clean board. Using culinary string tie two shoulder joints firmly to hold the two forequarters together. Borrow a second pair of hands at this stage.

Place forequarter into a large bowl, rib end facing upwards. Fill cavity with Roasted Vegetable Stuffing and pack in firmly. Place a small piece of Teflon, or greased aluminium foil, at each end to hold in stuffing. Using a long piece of string, tie forequarter lengthwise and widthwise to ensure stuffing doesn't fall out.

Place stuffed forequarter into the roasting tray and refrigerate overnight, or place into preheated oven. Roast for 30 minutes and then baste with pan juices. Decrease oven temperature to 180 °C. Cook lamb for a further 2 hours, basting with pan juices every 15 minutes or so. Because basting is important, set up a kitchen whiteboard with timings and delegate the basting to a zealous guest!

Temporarily remove from oven to tip off most of the fat collected in base of roasting pan. Remove fat for another use. Pour in wine and place back in oven to cook for a further 1–1½ hours or till shoulder end is cooked till medium–rare and stuffing is hot.

Remove lamb from oven. To rest, cover the tray with several heavy dry tea towels and sit at room temperature for 30–45 minutes. Tuck the tea towels under, rather than into, the tray. Resting will distribute juices evenly through the meat and greatly improve your ability to carve the lamb well.

Present lamb in a spectacular fashion on a groaning platter.

Double Lamb Forequarter with Roasted Vegetable Stuffing and Beetroot Jus – *continued from previous page*

Roasted Vegetable Stuffing	400 g (3) parsnips (peeled and cut into 1–1.5 cm dice)	and lightly mashed) (see page 162)	4 tbsp finely chopped oregano leaves
Enough to stuff 1 double lamb forequarter	400 g (2) kumara (peeled and cut into 1–1.5 cm dice)	400 g fresh white breadcrumbs (day-old bread crumbed in food processor)	1 tbsp flaky sea salt
240 g (2) red onions (peeled and diced)	flaky sea salt and freshly ground black pepper	2 tbsp lemon zest (long strands made with a lemon zester)	1½ tsp freshly ground black pepper
430 g (½ small) pumpkin (peeled and cut into 1–1.5 cm dice)	90 ml (6 tbsp) olive oil	120 g (14) sun-dried tomatoes (roughly chopped)	175 g unsalted butter (melted and cooled)
	24–32 cloves Roasted Garlic (squeezed from skin		

To carve lamb

Transfer lamb to a clean board. Using a sharp knife cut along each side of the backbone and lift bone away. Cut through the stuffing to make two separate halves. Turn the halves so the rounded side is uppermost.

At shoulder end, carve slices of meat to expose the shoulder blade. When you reach the blade bone, cut around and underneath to free it, and at the same time freeing the top shoulder bone. Lift out and cut away any meat still remaining on the bones.

Carve the shoulder into thick slices, incorporating stuffing with each slice.

Bone and carve the second shoulder in the same way.

Accompany with warmed Beetroot Jus.

This stuffing is delectable before you put it into the lamb, but once it is cooked and absorbs the lamb juices it is absolutely to die for.

To make Roasted Vegetable Stuffing

Preheat oven to 200 °C.

On 1 or 2 low-sided roasting trays, place onion, pumpkin, parsnip and kumara. Sprinkle each tray with salt and pepper and drizzle with oil. Toss vegetables to coat and spread vegetables out so they are not touching.

Place into preheated oven and cook for 10–12 minutes till vegetables are tender. Remove from oven and cool.

Into a large bowl place roasted vegetables, garlic, breadcrumbs, lemon zest, sun-dried tomatoes, oregano, salt and pepper. Pour in melted butter. Toss ingredients till stuffing holds together when squeezed in the hand.

Set aside in refrigerator till ready to use.

Mélange of Asparagus, Green Beans and Celery with Parsley Oil

Serves 8

flaky sea salt

320 g (16) asparagus (pinged and trimmed)

170–190 g (24) green beans (trimmed at stalk end)

200 g (2 stalks) celery (cut on a sharp angle to make long strips 1 cm wide)

45 ml (3 tbsp) Parsley Infused Olive Oil (see page 168)

flaky sea salt and freshly ground black pepper

Change the mélange to suit the seasons. Broccoli, broccolini, snow peas or fennel bulb could all be part of this dish.

Method

Bring a pot of lightly salted water to the boil.

Add asparagus and cook for 3–4 minutes or till al dente. Remove asparagus from water and, to keep asparagus hot and arrest further cooking, place into a container lined with a cold wet tea towel, and cover with the cold wet tea towel.

Bring water back to the boil. Add beans to pot and cook for 4–5 minutes or till al dente. Remove from water and add to container with asparagus.

Bring water back to the boil and add celery. Cook for 2–3 minutes or till al dente. Drain into a sieve and add celery to asparagus and beans. The vegetables will keep hot for up to 10 minutes if entirely wrapped in the cold wet tea towel.

When ready to serve, unwrap tea towel and tip vegetables into a bowl. Drizzle with Parsley Infused Olive Oil and season with salt and pepper to taste. Gently toss together and serve immediately.

Invest in a metal blanching basket for cooking vegetables. Place vegetables into the basket and then into a pot of lightly salted boiling water. Cook vegetables al dente; firm to the touch but soft to the bite. Lift basket of vegetables out of pot — so much more effective than draining vegetables with a pot lid.

Buttered Herbed Potatoes

Serves 8

1 kg graded small new potatoes (or 3 potatoes per person) (washed and scrubbed)

1 tsp flaky sea salt

1 large stalk mint

30 g (3 tbsp) unsalted butter (diced)

1 tbsp roughly chopped dill

1 tbsp roughly chopped Italian parsley leaves

1 tbsp roughly chopped chervil

flaky sea salt and freshly ground black pepper

This very simple idea for potatoes always plays to great applause. Serve with the Double Lamb Forequarter with Roasted Vegetable Stuffing (see page 119) or Frenched Lamb Racks with Lemon and Peppercorn Paste (see page 90) but actually fantastic with any meat dish. At spring and summer celebrations use Jersey Benne potatoes.

Method

Bring a saucepan half-filled with water to the boil. Add potatoes and remove water which is above the surface of the potatoes. Add salt and mint. Place a lid on pot and bring to the boil.

Reduce to a simmer, move lid slightly ajar and simmer for 15 minutes or till potatoes are fork tender.

Pour off water, remove mint and place back onto a low heat for a few minutes to remove residue water.

Remove from heat and add butter and herbs with salt and pepper to taste.

Tip into serving bowl and serve hot.

Christmas Crackers with Sweet Cherry Compote

Serves 8

190 g (¾ cup) cream cheese (at room temperature)

120 g (½ cup + 1 tbsp) sour cream

55 g (¼ cup) caster sugar

⅛ tsp vanilla bean paste or 1 tsp vanilla extract

1 tbsp finely grated lemon zest

1 egg (lightly beaten)

16 sheets filo pastry

100 g unsalted butter (melted)

30 g (3 tbsp) vanilla sugar

Sweet Cherry Compote (see page 170)

This dessert looks like a Christmas cracker but tastes like a warm cheesecake scented with vanilla and lemon. It is utterly delicious, and the cooking aromas will certainly build up dessert appetites. Vanilla bean paste, extract and sugar can be found at specialty food shops or in the specialty section of the supermarket.

Method

Place cream cheese into bowl of electric mixer and whisk till smooth.

Add sour cream, sugar, vanilla and lemon zest and mix till combined. With mixer still running slowly pour egg into cream cheese mixture and whisk till egg is combined and mixture is smooth.

Preheat oven to 170 °C.

Lay out one sheet filo pastry and cut in half to approximately 22 cm width.

Place one sheet of filo pastry on a clean work surface with narrowest edge facing you and, using a pastry brush, lightly butter. Repeat with three more layers of filo pastry. Lightly butter a 1-cm strip along edge that is furthest away from you.

Spoon a 50 g portion, or one-eighth of cream cheese mixture, into the centre of the filo pastry stack, but 2 cm from each end. Roll pastry loosely, keeping cream mix in the centre of the pastry and away from the ends. Repeat till you have made 8 cylinders.

Gently scrunch filo pastry at each end to make the cylinders look like Christmas crackers. Store in refrigerator for up to 1 day or bake immediately. When ready to bake, brush crackers with butter and sprinkle the cylinder sections of crackers with vanilla sugar.

Lightly grease a low-sided baking tray with baking spray or butter. Place crackers onto trays. Bake in preheated oven for 10–12 minutes till ends are golden and centre of pastry is crispy and puffed.

Serve with Sweet Cherry Compote and, if you wish, vanilla bean ice cream or vanilla-flavoured whipped cream.

Filo pastry sheets vary in size depending on the brand you use. With some brands you may get only one serving from each sheet and in that case you will need 32 sheets.

Summer Pudding

Serves 6–8

125 g (½ cup + 2 tbsp) sugar

125 g (1 cup) strawberries (hulled and sliced)

125 g (1 cup) blackcurrants (destalked)

190 g (1½ cups) blackberries

475 g (4 cups) raspberries

30 ml (2 tbsp) lemon juice

1 loaf thin slice white bread

whipped cream (for serving)

A simple-to-make and tried and true dessert for a summer celebration. Fresh berries are ideal but summer pudding can be made very adequately with frozen berries.

Method

Place sugar and strawberries in a pot over medium heat. Gently stir and cook for 5 minutes or till strawberries release their juices. Add remaining fruit and cook till the juice is released, but fruit still retains its shape. Remove from heat and place in a bowl to cool. Add lemon juice to taste.

Line a 1 litre (4 cup) pudding-shaped bowl with plastic wrap. Cut a bread circle the same size as base of bowl. Remove crusts from remainder of bread and cut bread into triangles.

Place bread circle on the base of bowl and pour 1½ cups berry mixture over bread. Fit bread triangles on top and pour on another 1½ cups of berry mixture. Continue till bowl is overflowing with berries and ending with bread.

Cover bowl with plastic wrap and place a tray or plate with weights (cans of baked beans would do the job) on top. Refrigerate overnight.

When ready to serve, invert pudding onto a serving platter, remove plastic wrap and serve with lashings of very cold whipped cream.

Ginger and Cashew Celebration Cake with Glacé Fruit

Makes one 20 cm round cake

125 g (¾ cup) raisins (roughly chopped)

190 g (1 cup + 3 tbsp) sultanas (roughly chopped)

40 g dried pineapple (roughly chopped)

40 g (13) dried apricots (roughly chopped)

45 g (2–3) dried figs (roughly chopped)

65 g (¼ cup + 2 tbsp) mixed peel

25 g (½ cup) preserved ginger (drained from syrup) (you will find in specialty section of your supermarket)

130 g (1 cup) raw cashews

65 ml (¼ cup) brandy

190 g (¾ cup) unsalted butter (diced and at room temperature) plus extra for greasing tin

190 g (¾ cup + 3 tbsp) caster sugar

3 whole eggs (separated)

3 egg yolks only

1 tsp finely grated lemon zest

¾ tsp ground cardamom

½ tsp ground cinnamon

½ tsp ground cloves

1½ tsp vanilla extract

1 tsp almond extract

1 tsp rose water

1½ tsp liquid honey

125 g (⅔ cup + 2 tbsp) semolina flour

210–260 g mixed glacé fruits (to decorate cake)

This is a cake packed with a wonderful variety of dried fruits and cashews, fragrant with preserved ginger and showy with a topping of glacé fruits. Don't reserve it just for Christmas.

Method

Into a large bowl place raisins, sultanas, pineapple, apricots, figs, peel, ginger and cashews. Pour in brandy, stir well and leave to macerate overnight.

Preheat oven to 140 °C.

Line base and sides of a 20 cm round tin with 2 layers of baking paper. Grease final layer of baking paper with butter.

Into the bowl of an electric mixer place butter and sugar and beat till light and fluffy. Add egg yolks (6 in total), one at a time, beating well between additions, till butter and yolks are combined.

Add lemon zest, cardamom, cinnamon, cloves, vanilla and almond extract, rose water and honey and mix well.

Add semolina flour and macerated dried fruits and mix thoroughly to incorporate.

Pour egg whites from separated eggs into a bowl and whisk till soft peaks form. Add half of the egg whites to cake mixture and gently fold to loosen mixture. Add remaining egg whites and gently fold to combine.

Spoon cake mixture into prepared cake tin and lightly spread out to make an even depth. Cut glacé fruits into thin slices horizontally and decorate the top of cake.

Fold 5 pages of newspaper in half and in half again to give you 20 layers of newspaper. Place this into oven and sit cake on top of newspaper stack.

Bake for 2 hours 20 minutes to 2 hours 30 minutes or till a cake skewer when inserted comes out clean. Keep checking cake every 30 minutes and if the cake is getting too dark on top, place 5 layers of newspaper on top for the final hour.

Remove from oven onto a cake rack. Completely cool cake before removing from tin.

Serve as soon as cake is cold or wrap well and store at room temperature for 3–4 weeks to serve later.

SIX

COFFEE

I had a wonderful aunt who was renowned for her baking. In middle-age there were a few years of her life when she didn't sleep, so every night those empty hours became baking time. In no time at all, the tins and the cupboards groaned with baking. She spent days entertaining visitors to use up the baking. They were given baking to take home and birds in her garden were fed royally. I always think of Auntie Elsie and her magnitude when I invite friends over for coffee and I bake one recipe, and it never makes it to the cupboard. Be welcoming, and whatever drink you are serving your guests, make sure they enjoy a tasty titbit created by the host.

132

Cheese Toasties

Serves 6

4 large eggs

300 g aged cheddar (grated)

2 spring onions (finely chopped, white part only)

flaky sea salt and freshly ground black pepper

Pide (Turkish-style flatbread) cut into 3 squares, approximately 8 cm, and each square cut horizontally through centre to equal 6 portions

Serve with soup, a glass of wine or indeed with coffee, at any time of the day or night. Choose a tangy cheddar for these toasties; the sort which grips you in the gills.

Method

Place eggs into a medium-size bowl and whisk lightly.

Add cheddar and spring onions with salt and pepper to taste and mix together.

Heat grill in oven. Place Pide, crust-side-up, on baking tray and place under grill.

Lightly toast crust-side of Pide. Turn Pide over and divide cheese mixture evenly onto untoasted cut sides. Cheese mixture should look very generous.

Place under grill and grill till cheese topping is puffy and lightly golden brown.

Cut each portion diagonally into two and serve hot with your favourite chutney.

Mint Tea

Makes 1 large jug

freshly picked mint

boiling water

A beverage made from steeping herbs is
called a tisane, infusion or, most simply, and
probably incorrectly, herb tea. Mint tea is
thirst quenching and the drink I reach for
when I have had my surfeit of caffeine for the
day. Plant mint in your garden, or in pots, so
you always have a supply for this refreshing
beverage.

Method

Pack a large jug half full with mint. If it is
a glass jug, it needs to be a sturdy version.
Place a long metal skewer or spoon into jug.
Pour boiling water into jug till jug is full. Stir
several times and leave to infuse for up to 5
minutes. Pour into glasses or cups to serve.

Rhubarb Friands with Crème Patisserie

Makes 12			Clarified Butter
150 g (1 cup) icing sugar (sifted)	155 ml (½ cup + 3 tbsp) egg whites (runny not whisked)	155 ml (½ cup + 3 tbsp) clarified butter (warm not hot)	Makes 155 ml
70 g (½ cup) flour (sifted)	2 tsp finely grated lemon zest	Crème Patisserie	170g butter
130 g (1¼ cups + 1 tbsp) ground almonds	300 g (2½ cups) rhubarb (diced)	extra icing sugar	

If you wish, freeze prepared but unbaked friands in their tins and when required bake from frozen. Bake at temperature specified in this recipe but allow 3–5 minutes additional baking time. Friand moulds are sold as trays of 6, which is a handy option for the freezer.

Method
Preheat oven to 180 °C. Grease 12 friand moulds with melted butter or baking spray.

Into a large bowl sift icing sugar and flour (so icing sugar and flour are sifted twice). Add ground almonds and combine.

Pour in egg whites, add lemon zest and rhubarb and stir to combine.

Slowly pour clarified butter into batter and gently fold till batter is entirely combined.

Divide batter in half. Evenly spoon one half into prepared moulds so moulds are half full. Place 2 teaspoons Crème Patisserie into centre of each mould and cover with remaining batter.

Place into preheated oven and bake for 20–25 minutes or till light golden brown and slightly pulling away from the sides of moulds. They should still be a little moist. Only when they are overcooked do they bounce back when prodded.

When cool enough to handle remove from moulds, sift extra icing sugar over friands and serve.

To make Clarified Butter
Place 170 g butter in a small saucepan and over a low heat melt butter slowly. Remove from heat and slowly pour butter through a fine sieve, leaving white milk solids in base of pot. Discard milk solids. The sieve will capture any scum off the top of the butter that has formed during the clarification process. Set aside to cool for 5–10 minutes before using, or store in the refrigerator for 2 to 3 weeks, depending on freshness of butter.

Crème Patisserie	3 egg yolks
Makes 350 ml	125 g (½ cup + 2 tbsp + 1 tsp) sugar
½ vanilla bean (cut lengthwise)	30 g (4 tbsp + ½ tsp) flour
250 ml (1 cup) milk	

Only about half of this will be required for Rhubarb Friands with Crème Patisserie. Reserve the remainder to use in fresh fruit tarts or as a filling for a cake.

To make Crème Patisserie
Place vanilla bean and milk into a saucepan and bring slowly to the boil. Remove from heat for 2 minutes.

In a separate bowl place egg yolks, sugar and flour and whisk till combined. Pour milk onto mixture, whisking as you pour.

Pour mixture back into saucepan and stir over a low heat till mixture comes to just below the boil. Pull pot slightly off heat to reduce to a simmer, or place a simmer mat under saucepan. Cook, while stirring, till mixture is thick.

Pour into a cold bowl and remove vanilla bean. Place plastic wrap directly onto surface of Crème Patisserie to prevent a skin forming.

Refrigerate till ready to use.

Rugelach with Apricot, Walnuts and Chocolate

Makes 16

190 g unsalted butter (diced and at room temperature)

60 g (⅓ cup + 1 tbsp) icing sugar

175 g cream cheese (diced and at room temperature)

½ tsp vanilla extract

280 g (2 cups) flour (sifted)

155 g (½ cup) apricot jam (aim for a chunky version)

60 g (½ cup) walnuts (chopped)

80 g (½ cup) dark (70%) chocolate (tablet, chopped)

1 egg (lightly beaten)

20 g (2 tbsp) sugar

Rugelach, a traditional Jewish pastry, is very satisfying with morning coffee. If you wish, prepare ahead of time, freeze unbaked, bake from frozen and just cook as many as you need at the time.

Method

To make pastry, place butter, icing sugar, cream cheese and vanilla extract into bowl of food processor fitted with a metal blade. Pulse just till ingredients begin to combine. Add half of the flour to ingredients in food processor bowl and pulse till just combined. Add remaining flour and pulse till pastry begins to form a ball.

Tip pastry onto a lightly floured bench and cut into 2 equal-sized pieces. Roll into balls and pat pastry into disc shapes. Wrap and chill for at least 2 hours or overnight.

Preheat oven to 180 °C. Lightly grease 1 or 2 baking trays with baking spray or melted butter.

Lightly flour a clean bench and roll one disc to 40 cm circle about 3 mm thick. Trim around outer edge to neaten.

Spread half of apricot jam over the round and sprinkle with half of walnuts and half of chocolate.

Cut round into 8 equal wedges like spokes in a wheel. Roll wedges up from the wide edge to the narrow point as you would a croissant. Place onto prepared baking tray and rest in refrigerator for 30 minutes. Repeat with second disc of pastry and remaining jam, walnuts and chocolate.

Brush each rugelach with egg and sprinkle with sugar.

Place into preheated oven and bake for 15–20 minutes or till golden brown and pastry is cooked through. Serve warm, or cool and warm to serve later.

Chocolate Hazelnut Biscuits

**Makes 30–35 little sand-
wich biscuits**

150 g (1 cup) hazelnuts

220 g (1 cup + 1 tbsp)
caster sugar

36 g (6 tbsp) cocoa
(preferably Dutched)

½ tsp baking powder

2 (¼ cup) egg whites

85 ml (⅓ cup) red wine

200 g dark (70%)
chocolate (tablet, chopped
then melted)

New Zealander Alice Pugh, resident in Italy,
introduced me to these biscuits nearly 20
years ago when she took the first-ever
class at our cooking school. The ingredient
list and method look weird but the recipe
really does work. The result is crispy, light
and flavoursome biscuits. You will be
baking 60–70 little biscuits to make 30–35
sandwich-style biscuits.

Method

Preheat oven to 150 °C. Grease several
baking trays with baking spray or oil, or for
preference cover trays with Teflon sheets.

Place hazelnuts on a tray and into oven to
cook for 5–7 minutes or till hazelnuts are
light brown and beginning to smell nutty.
Place into a tea towel or a drum sieve and rub
skins off. You don't need to be too fussy.

Into a food processor bowl fitted with metal
blade place hazelnuts and sugar and process
till fine.

Add cocoa, baking powder, egg whites and
red wine to food processor bowl and process
till just combined.

Drop batter in small teaspoonfuls onto trays
making sure there is space between biscuits
to allow for spreading. You may need to bake
biscuits in several oven-loads.

Place into preheated oven and bake for 10
minutes or till biscuits are slightly firm
around the edges but soft in the centre. As
biscuits cool, they crisp up.

Leave biscuits till they are just pliable
enough to remove from the trays and place
onto a rack to cool completely. If you leave
them on the tray to cool completely they will
stick to the greased tray, however they will
not stick to a Teflon sheet.

Sandwich 2 biscuits together, bottom-side to
bottom-side, with melted chocolate. When
chocolate has set store in an airtight container
at room temperature for up to 2 weeks.

Clockwise from above:

Sandra's Melt-In-Your-Mouth Fudge (see page 141)

Nougat Blanc (see page 140)

Chocolate Hazelnut Biscuits

Nougat Blanc

Makes 100 x 2 cm squares

2–3 sheets edible rice paper

1 tsp light olive oil or grapeseed oil

150 g (1 cup + 1 tbsp) blanched almonds (lightly roasted)

75 g (½ cup less 1 tbsp) mixed peel

75 g (½ cup + 2 tbsp) dried cranberries (craisins)

450 g (1⅓ cups) clover honey

2 (¼ cup) egg whites (at room temperature)

Serve small squares with coffee or line up bars on individual plates or a platter for dessert. Edible rice paper, designed for confectionery, can be found at specialty food or kitchen shops and at shops which specialise in Dutch products.

Method
Preheat oven to 150 °C.

Line the base of a 20 cm square cake tin with rice paper sheets. You may need to cut them to fit snugly, or slightly overlap them. Lightly oil sides of tin without getting oil onto rice paper sheets.

Place almonds, mixed peel and cranberries on small low-sided baking tray and cover with aluminium foil.

Place in oven for 7–10 minutes or till warm. Turn off oven and leave fruit and nuts in oven so they remain warm.

Pour honey into a saucepan and place over a medium heat. Stir till honey begins to boil. Remove from heat.

Place egg whites into a bowl and whisk till stiff peaks form. Pour into honey and stir together.

Return pot to a low heat. I like to place a simmer mat under the saucepan at this stage. Stir continuously for 10–15 minutes or till mixture reaches a toffee-like consistency. You can test this by dropping a half-teaspoon of nougat into a jug of cold water and leaving for 2 minutes. The nougat should roll easily between your fingers into a ball and be quite firm.

Add warm nuts and fruits, in two or three lots, and stir quickly to combine.

Spoon nougat into prepared tin and push into the sides. Cover top with a second piece of rice paper and press gently to smooth the top.

Leave to sit at room temperature till completely cold. Best stored as one piece in an airtight container at room temperature. Nougat will keep for 2–3 weeks uncut.

Remove nougat from tin by running a cold wet knife along the sides of the tin and shake out onto a board. Cut nougat into portions on the day you are serving it.

Sandra's Melt-In-Your-Mouth Fudge

Makes 56 x 2.5 cm
squares

100 g butter (roughly
chopped)

26 g (2 tbsp) golden syrup

395 g (1 tin) sweetened
condensed milk

200 g (1 cup) brown sugar

80 g dark (70%) chocolate
(tablet, chopped)

80 g white chocolate
(tablet, chopped)

160 g dark (70%)
chocolate (tablet, chopped
and melted) for icing

My friend and ex-neighbour Sandra Cottle, with her husband John, owns The Woolshed Homestay in Scotsmans Valley in the Waikato, and likes to give guests an edible gift. Sandra's Russian Fudge didn't work one day and from her mistake comes this truly divine, melt-in-your-mouth fudge.

Method
Line base of a 20 cm square tin with a Teflon sheet or baking paper cut to measure.

Place butter into a medium-size saucepan over a medium heat and stir till only just melted.

Add golden syrup, condensed milk and sugar. Cook over a gentle heat, stirring continuously for 4–5 minutes, till sugar is dissolved. It is very important not to rush this stage. The mixture should now be smooth and glossy looking.

Place a simmer mat under saucepan and, over a very gentle heat, simmer mixture for 14–16 minutes, stirring every 3–4 minutes. Maintain a vigil, as left without stirring the texture will quickly change from smooth to gritty.

Remove saucepan from heat. The mixture should still look smooth and glossy. Add first measure of dark chocolate and then white chocolate. Stir well till chocolate has melted.

Pour fudge mixture into prepared tin. Using your hand, push it down very firmly so it is spread into the corners. Place in refrigerator, chill till set, then proceed to the next step before fudge becomes very cold. If you allow it to become very cold then bring back to room temperature before proceeding to the next step.

Pour melted chocolate over top of fudge. Shake tin to spread chocolate without touching chocolate. At room temperature allow just to set, approximately 30 minutes.

Remove fudge from tin and, if you enjoy precision, mark cutting lines with a ruler and cut fudge into 2.5 cm squares. Wipe knife as you go, but don't wet or heat knife in between cuts.

Store in an airtight container in refrigerator till required. Best eaten at room temperature within 7 days.

Rocky Road

Makes 25 x 4 cm squares

1 tsp icing sugar

1 tsp cornflour

1 x recipe Marshmallow

65 g (½ cup) pistachios (lightly roasted)

50 g (⅓ cup) dried cranberries (craisins) (firmly packed)

75 g dark (70%) chocolate (tablet, chopped and melted)

100 g white chocolate (tablet, chopped and melted)

Marshmallow

12 g (1 tbsp) gelatine powder

65 ml (¼ cup) water

200 g (1 cup) sugar

125 ml (½ cup) water

1 tsp vanilla extract

A familiar but updated sweetmeat. The addition of tangy dried cranberries reduces the sweetness so gives this Rocky Road adult appeal.

Method

Grease with baking spray, or oil, a 20 cm square cake tin. Place icing sugar and cornflour in a small bowl and combine. Place into a small fine sieve and lightly shake into and up sides of tin. Shake out any excess.

Pour marshmallow into prepared tin and spread to corners. Sprinkle pistachios and cranberries on top of marshmallow.

Drizzle pistachios and cranberries with dark chocolate and repeat with white chocolate. Using the point of a skewer, swirl two chocolates together. Leave at room temperature to set for a minimum of 2 hours.

Portion and serve Rocky Road, or store in the whole piece in an airtight container at room temperature for up to 4 days.

To make Marshmallow

Place gelatine and first measure of water in a small bowl and leave for 10 minutes or till gelatine powder has absorbed the water. Place sugar and second measure of water in a small pot. Heat gently, stirring constantly till sugar dissolves. Pour gelatine into sugar mixture and bring to the boil. Boil steadily for 9 minutes.

Remove from heat and, working quickly, pour gelatine mixture into a bowl of an electric mixer, add vanilla extract and whisk till thick and white but still pourable.

Proceed with Rocky Road recipe, or pour into tray or moulds and leave to set.

To melt chocolate

Place dark chocolate into a bowl and place bowl over a pot one-quarter filled with water. Use a pot the bowl fits into snugly. Simmer on a gentle heat till chocolate is three-quarters melted. Remove from heat and stir till chocolate is completely melted. Cool.

Rocky Road traditionally has pink and white marshmallow in it. If you wish, colour this marshmallow pink or even pale green.

Chocolate Mice

Makes 15 father mice and 15 mother mice

⅔ recipe Dark Chocolate Truffle Mix

300–350 g (15) Medjool dates (available from fresh produce section of supermarket)

115–125g (15) prunes

60 silver cachous (tiny sugar pellets used to decorate cakes)

10–15 g (60) sliced almond pieces

1 licorice strap

150 g dark (70%) chocolate (tablet, chopped and melted)

Dark Chocolate Truffle Mix

Makes 180 g mix or enough for 60 petite truffles

160 g dark (70%) chocolate (tablet, chopped)

160 ml (⅔ cup less 1 tsp) cream

5 ml (1 tsp) dark rum or liqueur such as Grand Marnier

I loathe mice with such a passion I scream on sight. Chefs in our kitchen created this sweetmeat as part of a supper for the ballet *Cinderella* and could hardly wait to taunt me with them.

Method
To make father mice, roll 5 g (1 teaspoon) truffle mix into a cylindrical shape. Repeat to make 15 cylindrical rolls.

Remove stones from dates by cutting down one side of each date to open it up.

Place shaped truffle mix inside each date and close dates. Place dates cut-side down onto a tray. Mould each date to form a mouse body by pressing thumb and forefinger into one end, leaving indentations for eyes and nose. Using a small knife make two slits just behind the indentations (these will be for the ears). Press 2 cachous into the indentations for eyes, and slide 2 almond slices into the slits for the ears.

Cut licorice into 8 cm strips and cut each strip into very thin lengths to create tails.

Lay tails on a foil-lined tray with 5 cm gaps between each tail.

Dip tail end of each mouse halfway into melted chocolate and sit directly on top of licorice tail.

To make mother mice, repeat the same process using prunes and using 3 g of truffle mix to fill each prune.

Refrigerate mice till they are set. Use immediately or store in an airtight container in a cool dark place for 2–3 days.

To make Dark Chocolate Truffle Mix
Place chocolate in a large bowl. Pour cream into a saucepan set over a medium heat and bring to the boil. Remove from heat and sit for 2 minutes. Pour cream onto chocolate. Stir till chocolate has melted and mixture has combined. Add rum and mix together.

Leave mixture at room temperature for 2–3 hours or, particularly in warm weather, cool and place in refrigerator for 45 minutes, till it is malleable.

Mango, Orange and Passionfruit Cake

Makes 1 x 25 cm cake

225 g unsalted butter (diced and at room temperature)

400 g (2 cups) sugar

2 eggs (lightly beaten)

10 ml (2 tsp) vanilla extract

4 tsp finely grated orange zest

420 g (3 cups) flour

1 tsp cream of tartar

½ tsp table salt

55 g (½ cup) roughly chopped macadamias

2 oranges (peeled and roughly chopped)

approx 50 ml (3 tbsp + 1 tsp) water

2 tsp baking soda

35 g (½ cup) thread coconut

400 g (1–2) mangoes (peeled and flesh cut into 1 cm dice)

125 ml (½ cup) Passionfruit Syrup (see page 169)

whipped cream to accompany

This moist and flavoursome cake is great for morning or afternoon tea. It's a cake with substance! It's the sort of cake you can take to a friend or have in the tin just in case you receive visitors.

Method

Grease with baking spray, or oil, the base and sides of one 25 cm round springform tin. Line base and sides with 2 layers of baking paper.

Preheat oven to 175 °C.

Place butter and sugar into bowl of an electric mixer fitted with a paddle attachment. Beat butter and sugar till pale and creamy.

Add eggs, a little at a time, mixing between additions, till eggs are incorporated and mixture is light and fluffy.

Add vanilla extract and orange zest and mix to combine.

Sift flour, cream of tartar and salt into a separate bowl. Add to butter mixture, mixing till just combined. Add macadamias and stir in.

Place oranges into food processor bowl fitted with a metal blade and purée. Pour into a 250 ml (1 cup) jug. You should have approximately 200 ml of purée. Top the jug up with water to make 250 ml (1 cup) purée. Add baking soda to purée and as the baking soda is now active, working very quickly, stir into cake batter. Mix to combine.

Still working very quickly, pour cake batter into prepared tin and sprinkle with coconut. Evenly scatter mango over coconut. Using a pastry brush in a dabbing motion rather than brushing, coat mango evenly with Passionfruit Syrup.

Still working very quickly place cake into preheated oven and bake for 1 hour 20 minutes or till centre of cake is cooked and mango is just staring to colour.

Remove from oven to cake cooling rack. Serve warm or cool and serve that day or within 3–4 days. Store at room temperature.

SEVEN

CONDIMENTS

It is the little things that really make the difference in cooking and in entertaining. Like the icing on the cake; the pickle is to the burger, the jus to the lamb and the dressing to the fruit. Mix and match condiments and dishes to use up what you have on hand and what is in season. Steak, salad and spuds can suddenly become Rib-eye Steak with Beetroot and Horseradish Condiment, Green Salad with Raspberry Vinaigrette and Potatoes with Herbed Caper Sauce. Suddenly you have a menu rather than just a meal. Taste as you create and taste again as you serve, as food is all about flavour.

Basil Pesto

Sun-dried Tomato Pesto

Makes 315 g

2 cloves garlic (peeled)

75 g (½ cup) pine nuts

90 g (1½ cups) basil leaves

35 g (½ cup) grated Parmesan

85 ml (⅓ cup) olive oil

flaky sea salt and freshly ground black pepper

juice of 1 lemon

Makes 300 g

2 cloves garlic (peeled)

25 g (3 tbsp) pine nuts

195 g (1 cup plus 1 tbsp) sun-dried tomatoes (drained and chopped – reserve oil)

½ cup roughly chopped Italian parsley leaves

juice of 2 limes

½ small red chilli (chopped)

½ tbsp tomato paste

20 ml reserved sun-dried tomato oil

flaky sea salt and freshly ground black pepper

When basil is plentiful make loads of pesto and freeze.

When there is a surfeit of parsley make this pesto and freeze.

Method

Into bowl of a food processor, fitted with a metal blade, place garlic, pine nuts, basil and Parmesan.

Through feed tube, with processor going, slowly add olive oil.

Add salt and pepper with lemon juice to suit your taste.

Method

Into bowl of a food processor, fitted with a metal blade, place garlic, pine nuts, sun-dried tomatoes, parsley, lime juice, chilli and tomato paste and process till mixture resembles a paste.

Through feed tube, with processor going, slowly add reserved sun-dried tomato oil.

Add salt and pepper to suit your taste.

Sandwich Mayonnaise

Makes 625 ml

4 egg yolks

1 garlic clove

½ tsp flaky sea salt and ¼ tsp freshly ground black pepper

2 tsp wholegrain mustard

juice of 1½ lemons

65 ml (¼ cup) canola, grapeseed or salad oil

440 ml (1¾ cups) canola, grapeseed or salad oil

This thick mayonnaise was named on account of its job. It was designed to NOT ooze out of a sandwich when a guest takes a bite.

Method

Into bowl of a food processor, fitted with a metal blade, place egg yolks, garlic, salt, pepper, mustard, lemon juice and the first measure of oil. Process till smooth.

Place second measure oil into a jug and very slowly pour through the feed tube with the machine going.

Season to taste. Store in the refrigerator tightly covered for up to 5 days.

Mustard Mayonnaise

Makes 625 ml

4 egg yolks

flaky sea salt and freshly ground pepper

4 tbsp grain mustard

1 tbsp Dijon mustard

juice of 1 lemon

500 ml (2 cups) grapeseed or canola oil

This mustard-flavoured mayonnaise is perfect with a burger or to dip French fries into.

Method

Into bowl of a food processor, fitted with a metal blade, place egg yolks, salt, pepper, mustards, lemon juice and ¼ cup oil. Process till smooth.

With food processor running, very slowly pour remaining oil through the feed tube.

Season to taste.

Store in refrigerator covered for up to 7 days.

If the mayonnaise is too thick for its purpose, thin down by slowly pouring 1 tablespoon boiling water through feed tube while food processor is running.

Caperberry Vinaigrette

Makes 200 ml

100 ml (⅓ cup plus 1 tbsp) extra virgin olive oil

60 ml (4 tbsp) lime juice

15 ml (1 tbsp) mirin

2 tbsp finely chopped rinsed pickled gherkins

8 caperberries (rinsed, stalks removed and roughly chopped)

1 tbsp finely chopped dill

1 tsp flaky sea salt

¼ tsp freshly ground black pepper

Enjoy with roast beef or potatoes, warm cauliflower or as an accompaniment to fish.

Method

Into a high-sided bowl place oil, lime juice, mirin, gherkins, caperberries, dill, salt and pepper.

Whisk till well combined and a temporary emulsion is formed. Store in refrigerator till required or for up to 3 days.

Serve at room temperature. Whisk again before serving.

Salsa Verde

Makes 350 g

100 g sourdough bread (crusts removed and diced)

30 ml (2 tbsp) red wine vinegar

150 g (approximately 5 cups lightly packed) finely chopped Italian parsley leaves

3 anchovies (rinsed and chopped) (white for preference)

1 clove garlic (crushed)

35 g (3 tbsp) capers (drained and rinsed)

500 ml (2 cups) extra virgin olive oil

flaky sea salt and freshly ground black pepper

This cold sauce uses a large amount of Italian parsley and the secret to its success is to blend it at very high speed for as short a time as possible so as not to compromise the fresh taste of the parsley. This version of Salsa Verde is adapted from a recipe we prepared for New York chef, Brad Farmerie, from Public Restaurant.

Method

Into a large bowl place bread and drizzle with vinegar. Leave to soak for 15 minutes.

Add parsley, anchovies, garlic, capers and two-thirds of the oil.

Place into blender and blend on high speed till purée is reached.

Remove from blender to bowl and add remaining oil. Stir in and refrigerate till required. Season to taste.

Store covered in refrigerator for up to 5 days but serve at room temperature.

Clockwise from top left:

Salsa Verde (see page 153)

Caesar Salad Dressing

Herbed Caper Sauce

Caesar Salad Dressing

Makes 250 ml

1 tsp flaky sea salt

¾ tsp freshly ground black pepper

2 cloves garlic (peeled and crushed)

½ tsp mustard powder

1¼ tsp Dijon mustard

1 tbsp + 1 tsp chopped tarragon leaves

1 tsp lemon juice

30 ml (2 tbsp) tarragon vinegar

125 ml (½ cup) extra virgin olive oil

1 egg

If you wish add rinsed anchovies, traditional in a Caesar dressing. This version, very fragrant with tarragon, is divine with the salad but also as an accompaniment to egg or chicken dishes.

Method

Place all ingredients in a non-reactive bowl and whisk to combine. Store in refrigerator for up to 3 days.

Herbed Caper Sauce

Makes 375 ml

75 ml (5 tbsp) water

30 ml (2 tbsp) malt vinegar

2 slices of white bread (crusts removed, chopped)

4 anchovy fillets (rinsed and chopped)

½ cup chopped Italian parsley leaves

juice of ½ lemon

1 tbsp capers in brine (drained and rinsed)

20 g (5) green olives (rinsed and pitted)

1 clove garlic (peeled)

70 g (½ cup) pine nuts (lightly roasted)

2 hard boiled egg yolks

90 ml (6 tbsp) olive oil

flaky sea salt and freshly ground black pepper

This is absolutely delicious spread on crostini, served in a bowl with seafood or tossed through a potato salad.

Method

Place water and vinegar into a bowl. Place bread into bowl and allow to soak for 2–3 minutes. Squeeze bread dry.

Into food processor bowl fitted with a metal blade place bread, anchovy fillets, parsley, lemon juice, capers, olives, garlic, pine nuts and egg yolks. Process till smooth.

With processor running, slowly pour in olive oil through feed tube. Add salt and pepper to taste.

Chilli Saffron Vinaigrette

Makes 135 ml

65 ml (¼ cup) white wine vinegar

⅓ tsp chilli flakes

½ clove garlic (crushed)

3 saffron threads

½ tsp caster sugar

65 ml (⅓ cup) olive oil

flaky sea salt and freshly ground black pepper

Drizzle over potato salad, Mediterranean vegetables or over grilled fish.

Method

Into a small pot pour white wine vinegar and heat over a medium heat till steaming.

Add chilli flakes, garlic and saffron and set aside for 30 minutes for flavours to infuse.

Add sugar and oil, whisk together and add salt and pepper to taste. Serve immediately or store in refrigerator for 3–4 days.

David's Tangy Lemon Dressing

Makes 360 ml

250 ml (1 cup) grapeseed oil

2½ tsp finely grated lemon zest

50 ml (2 tbsp + 2 tsp) lemon juice

2 lemons (peeled and segmented)

30 g (2 tbsp) honey (gently warmed till runny)

½ tsp flaky sea salt

⅛ tsp white pepper

This exceptionally tasty dressing comes courtesy of my ex-Marbles Restaurant partner, David Jordan. If you wish, substitute orange for lemon for an excellent orange dressing.

Method

Into a blender or food processor bowl fitted with a metal blade, place oil, zest, juice and lemon segments, honey, salt and pepper and process till smooth.

Pour into a container, cover and store in refrigerator for up to 5 days.

Clockwise from above:

Chilli Saffron Vinaigrette

David's Tangy Lemon Dressing

Yoghurt, Feta and Dill Dressing (see page 158)

Yoghurt, Feta and Dill Dressing

Makes 315 ml

250 ml (1 cup) Greek-style yoghurt

60 g creamy-style feta (crumbled)

1 tbsp roughly chopped dill

1 tbsp finely chopped chives

½ tsp finely grated lemon zest

Serve in a small bowl alongside falafel, vegetable fritters, steamed broccoli or lamb chops.

Method

Into a small bowl place yoghurt, feta, dill, chives and zest and combine.

Stir well and leave to sit at room temperature for at least 1 hour for flavours to infuse. Serve immediately or store in the refrigerator for up to 3 days. Serve at room temperature.

Raspberry Vinaigrette

Makes 60 ml

45 ml (3 tbsp) extra virgin olive oil

15 ml (1 tbsp) raspberry vinegar

flaky sea salt and freshly ground black pepper

Serve with leafy greens, pumpkin or root vegetable salads.

Method

Into a small bowl place oil and vinegar, with salt and pepper to taste. Whisk well before using.

Quince Jelly Dressing

Makes 265 ml

65 ml (¼ cup) red wine vinegar

125 ml (½ cup) grapeseed oil

¼ tsp flaky sea salt

pinch white pepper

65 ml (¼ cup) quince jelly (gently melted and cooled)

15 ml (1 tbsp) runny honey

A dressing recipe courtesy of David Jordan from Taste restaurant in Khandallah, Wellington. David has the best ideas for dressings. Serve this dressing with spinach salad or any dish involving blue cheese.

Method

Into the bowl of a blender or a food processor fitted with a metal blade, place vinegar, oil, salt, pepper, quince jelly and honey. Blend or process till combined.

Store in an airtight container in the refrigerator for up to 2 weeks. Bring to room temperature before serving.

Lime Wasabi Dressing

Makes 150 ml

65 ml (¼ cup) olive oil

45 ml (3 tbsp) lime juice

2 tsp finely grated lime zest

15 ml (1 tbsp) floral-flavoured honey such as Tawari

2 tsp wasabi paste

½ tsp kelp pepper

½ tsp flaky sea salt

A refreshing dressing to accompany salmon, scallops, scampi or fish.

Method

Into a small bowl place olive oil, lime juice and zest, honey, wasabi, kelp pepper and salt. Whisk ingredients together.

Serve immediately or cover and store in the refrigerator for up to 4 days. Rewhisk to serve.

Clockwise from top left:

Lime Wasabi Dressing (see page 159)

Beetroot Jus

Citrus Crème Fraîche

Citrus Crème Fraîche

Makes 210 ml

200 g crème fraîche

½ tsp finely grated lemon zest

¼ tsp finely grated lime zest

1 tsp lemon juice

1 tsp lime juice

¼ tsp flaky sea salt

This zesty savoury cream is a simple but very worthy accompaniment to fish, salmon, prawns and scampi.

Method

Into a small bowl place crème fraîche, lemon and lime zests, lemon and lime juices and salt and mix together.

Store covered in refrigerator for up to 3 days.

Beetroot Jus

Makes 270 ml

125 ml (½ cup) beef stock

375 ml (1½ cups) beetroot juice (you require 1 kg of peeled fresh beetroot to make the juice)

15 ml (1 tbsp) redcurrant jelly

½ tsp balsamic vinegar

flaky sea salt and freshly ground black pepper

Buy beetroot juice from a juice bar and as it has a short shelf life and freeze till you are ready to make this jus. Alternatively make beetroot juice in a vegetable juicer. This is a lovely fresh-tasting sauce with lamb or venison.

Method

Into a small pot pour beef stock and, over a medium–high heat, reduce by half.

Add beetroot juice and reduce to approximately 1 cup in volume.

Remove from heat and stir in redcurrant jelly and balsamic vinegar with salt and pepper to taste.

Caramelised Onions

Makes 360 g

140 g unsalted butter (diced)

450 g (2½) medium red onions (cut into 1–1.5 cm wedges)

70 g (⅓ cup) caster sugar

15 ml (1 tbsp) white wine vinegar

1 tbsp finely chopped thyme leaves

flaky sea salt and freshly ground black pepper

Very tasty with cold meats, in sandwiches or rolls, as a topping on steak or with sausages.

Method

In a heavy-based frying pan set over a medium heat place butter and melt. Increase heat, add onions and cook for 8–10 minutes till soft and beginning to colour.

Reduce heat to medium, add sugar, vinegar and thyme with salt and pepper to suit your taste. Cook for a further 8–10 minutes, or till onions are caramelised and golden.

This version has more butter than usual as it is designed for the Roasted Winter Vegetable Tart Tartin (see page 72). Decrease quantity of butter by half if for another use.

Roasted Garlic

Yield depends on size of garlic bulbs and cloves

3–4 bulbs of garlic

extra virgin olive oil

1 tbsp fresh thyme leaves (optional)

flaky sea salt and freshly ground black pepper

Have on hand to incorporate into mashed potato, pasta dishes, stuffings or to spread on crostini.

Method

Preheat oven to 180 °C.

Trim top quarter off whole garlic bulbs to expose cloves. To avoid bitterness place in a small saucepan of water set over a medium heat, bring to the boil and cook for 10 minutes. Drain. Discard any loose skin and puncture sides and top with a fork.

Place in a small ceramic dish and drizzle generously with oil then sprinkle with thyme, salt and pepper.

Place in oven and roast for 40 minutes or till cloves start popping out of skins.

When garlic has cooled or when you are ready to use it, squeeze pulp out from skin. Store roasted bulbs or squeezed-out pulp covered in olive oil in refrigerator for up to 3 weeks.

Zucchini Pickle

Makes 3 x 270 ml jars

225 g green zucchini

225 g yellow scallopini or zucchini

150 g (2 small) red onions (peeled)

2 tbsp flaky sea salt

½ cup ice cubes

water to cover

500 ml (2 cups) cider vinegar

200 g (1 cup) sugar

1½ tsp dry mustard

1 tsp black mustard seeds

1 tsp yellow mustard seeds

1 tsp dill seeds

½ tsp turmeric

Perfect with a burger or hot dog and very, very nice with tangy cheddar. This pickle is based on a recipe by Digby Law from *Pickle & Chutney Cookbook* published by Hodder Moa.

Method

Slice zucchini, scallopini and red onion very finely. A mandoline makes the task very straightforward.

Into a large, shallow dish place zucchini, scallopini and onion. Add salt and toss to coat. Add ice cubes with water to cover. Stir to dissolve salt and leave at room temperature for 1 hour.

Taste a slice of zucchini; it should be slightly salty and softened. Drain and remove any remaining ice cubes.

Dry vegetables thoroughly between tea towels or in a salad spinner as excess water will dilute the flavour. Place vegetables into a large bowl.

Into a pot place vinegar, sugar, mustard, mustard seeds, dill seeds and turmeric. Bring to the boil, reduce heat and simmer for 3 minutes. Set aside till lukewarm. If pickling liquid is too hot the vegetables will become limp, however if pickling mixture is cold the vegetables will not take on all its flavours.

Pour over vegetables and stir well.

Transfer vegetables to sterilised jars. Cover and refrigerate for at least a day before serving or refrigerate for up to 6 months.

Clockwise from top left:

Cucumber and Mint Relish

Caperberry Vinaigrette (see page 153) (left) and
  Beetroot and Horseradish Condiment

Zucchini Pickle (see page 163)

Cucumber and Mint Relish

Makes 6 x 270 ml jars

400 g (3 cups) cucumber (halved lengthwise, seeds removed and diced)

1½ tbsp table salt

190 ml (¾ cup plus 1 tsp) white vinegar

100 g (½ large) finely diced onion

215 g (1 large) red capsicum (finely diced)

225 g (1 cup + 2 tbsp) white sugar

⅔ cup roughly chopped mint leaves

1 tsp yellow or brown mustard seeds

pinch cayenne pepper

1 tsp dill seeds

1½ tbsp cornflour

You can eat relish immediately or store in a cool dark place for up to 4 months. Unlike chutney, relish does not improve with age. This version is fantastic with lamb.

Method

In a bowl place cucumber, sprinkle with salt. Barely cover with cold water. Allow to stand overnight.

Drain and rinse cucumber.

Into a large saucepan place cucumber, vinegar, onion, red capsicum, sugar, mint, mustard seeds, cayenne pepper and dill seeds. Bring to the boil, stirring constantly.

Mix cornflour with a little water and stir into relish. Simmer for 2–3 minutes, or till cornflour is cooked through.

Pour into hot, sterilised jars and seal. Eat immediately or store in a cool dark place for up to 4 months.

Beetroot and Horseradish Condiment

Makes 200 g

15 g (2 tbsp) very finely chopped onion

1½ tsp lemon juice

1 tsp sugar

45 ml (3 tbsp) sour cream

2 tsp prepared horseradish sauce

flaky sea salt and freshly ground black pepper

150 g cooked beetroot (peeled and grated) (use coarse Microplane grater)

Dollop onto roast beef, barbecued steak or use as a spread in open sandwiches.

Method

Place onion, lemon juice, sugar, sour cream, horseradish sauce, salt and pepper into a small bowl. Stir well till combined and sour cream is smooth.

Add beetroot and mix well. Serve immediately or store in refrigerator for up to 2 days. Serve at room temperature.

Cashew Dipping Sauce

Makes 200 ml

1 clove garlic (crushed)

¼ cup cashews (toasted)

1 tsp sherry vinegar

30 ml (2 tbsp) lemon juice

1 tsp manuka honey (warmed to a liquid)

½ tsp flaky sea salt

65 ml (¼ cup) extra virgin olive oil

1 medium-size tomato (skinned, seeded and diced)

Use as an accompaniment to battered fish, barbecued prawns, scallops or with vegetable crudités.

Method

Into the bowl of a food processor fitted with a metal blade place garlic, cashews, vinegar, lemon juice, honey and salt. Process till nuts are coarsely chopped.

With the food processor running slowly pour in the oil through the feed tube and process till well combined.

Pour sauce into a small bowl, add tomato and stir to combine.

Serve immediately or store in refrigerator for up to 3 days. Serve at room temperature.

Spring Herb Dressing

Makes 360 ml

90 ml (6 tbsp) verjuice

45 ml (3 tbsp) lemon juice

9 capers in brine (rinsed and finely chopped)

1½ tsp sea salt

¾ tsp freshly ground black pepper

190 ml (¾ cup) olive oil

3 tbsp Italian parsley leaves

3 tbsp dill leaves

A light but acidic dressing with pronounced herb flavours. Serve with salad, over vegetables or potatoes or drizzled onto fish.

Method

Into a small bowl place verjuice, lemon juice, capers, salt and pepper and combine. Slowly pour in olive oil while whisking till dressing has emulsified.

Use immediately or refrigerate for up to 7 days.

Add herb leaves and stir in just prior to serving.

Clockwise from above:

Cashew Dipping Sauce

Spring Herb Dressing

Parsley Infused Olive Oil (see page 168)

Parsley Infused Olive Oil

Makes 135 ml

1 litre (4 cups) water

1 tsp flaky sea salt

2 cups firmly packed curly parsley (stalks removed)

250 ml (1 cup) olive oil

Drizzle over green vegetables, baked potatoes in their jackets or grilled fish.

Method

In a medium-size saucepan place water and salt and bring to the boil. Add parsley and blanch for 15 seconds.

Drain parsley and plunge into chilled water. Drain again. Place parsley into a clean tea towel, roll up and gently squeeze out as much moisture as possible.

Into a blender place parsley and oil. Process on high for 2–3 minutes or till mixture is very green and smooth.

Pour oil through a muslin-lined sieve set over a bowl. Let drain for at least 1 hour. For the clearest oil let it drip undisturbed; do not be tempted to squeeze muslin and parsley.

Discard contents of sieve and use oil immediately, or store in a sealed bottle in refrigerator for up to 1 month.

Lemon Infused Olive Oil

Makes 250 ml

250 ml (1 cup) light olive oil (this is available at supermarkets and 'light' refers to the flavour)

¼ cup finely grated lemon zest

Drizzle over hot green vegetables. It is particularly special with asparagus or beans.

Method

Place oil and lemon zest into a bowl. Stir, cover and place in refrigerator for up to 4 days so that the zest can infuse the oil.

Strain through muslin, discard zest and store oil in a sterilised jar in refrigerator for up to 4 weeks.

Passionfruit Syrup

Makes 140 ml

125 ml (½ cup) passionfruit pulp (scoop passionfruit to obtain pulp or purchase frozen passionfruit pulp)

65 g (¼ cup) caster sugar

Drizzle onto cakes or muffins, pour over vanilla ice cream, or use as base for non-alcoholic punch.

Method

In a small pot place passionfruit pulp and sugar. Set over low heat and stir till sugar is dissolved.

Bring to the boil, reduce heat to medium, and allow to simmer for 5 minutes till pulp becomes a thick syrup.

Amaretto Dressing

Makes 475 ml

375 ml (1½ cups) sour cream

125 g (½ cup + 2 tbsp) brown sugar

45 ml (3 tbsp) Amaretto (almond-flavoured liqueur)

Serve with fresh fruit salad, grilled bananas or pineapple or bowls of fresh berries. Amaretto is known as the 'liqueur of love'.

Method

Into bowl place all ingredients and whisk till smooth.

Store covered in refrigerator for up to 5 days.

Sweet Cherry Compote

170

Makes 350 ml

250 ml (1 cup) pinot noir

75 ml (¼ cup + 2 tsp) orange juice (juice of 1 orange)

100 ml (⅓ cup + 1 tbsp) redcurrant jelly

20 g (2 tbsp) sugar

1½ tsp potato or rice flour

1 tsp water

200 g (30) cherries (fresh or frozen, and pitted)

4 tsp cherry brandy

Serve over vanilla ice cream, with baked cheesecake or dollop onto cream-filled sponge cake.

Method

Into a small saucepan set over a low heat, pour red wine, orange juice and redcurrant jelly. Add sugar and stir till sugar and jelly are dissolved.

Bring to the boil, reduce heat and simmer for 10–15 minutes till reduced by one-third and syrupy.

In a small bowl place potato or rice flour. Add water and stir till a thick paste is obtained. Add to sauce and stir for 5 minutes or till thickened.

Add cherries and cherry brandy and simmer for a further 5 minutes.

Serve immediately or store in refrigerator for up to 4 days. Serve warm or cold.

Dried Figs in Red Wine

Serves 8

375 ml (1½ cups) red wine
(merlot or cabernet)

150 g (8) dried figs (stalks
trimmed)

45 ml (3 tbsp) liquid honey

1½ tsp balsamic vinegar

**Fill jars with these figs and store in the
refrigerator to serve with terrines, cold
meats, brie-style and curd-style cheeses.**

Method

Into a small pot pour wine and bring to
boiling point. Remove from heat and add figs.
Leave to soak for 30 minutes.

Add honey and balsamic vinegar to the pot
and return pot to a medium heat. Stir till
honey is dissolved then bring to the boil.

Reduce heat to a simmer and cook for 20
minutes or till figs are plump and juicy and
syrup is thick and sticky. Cool.

Serve figs at room temperature with a
spoonful of syrup. Store in refrigerator for up
to 1 month.

Index

A

Almonds, Chilli-spiced with Cumin 21

Amaretto and Chocolate Cheesecake, Baked 52

Amaretto Dressing 169

Apple and Caramelised Walnut Tart 75

Apples, Baked Gala, with Blackcurrants 78

Apple Syrup Marinade 68

Asparagus, Green Beans and Celery, Mélange of 121

B

Baked Chocolate and Amaretto Cheesecake 52

Baked Gala Apples with Blackcurrants 78

Baked Pears in Verjuice with Vanilla 101

Baking and slices

Chocolate Hazelnut Biscuits 138

Chocolate Mice 144

Ginger and Cashew Celebration Cake with Glacé Fruit 128

Mango, Orange and Passionfruit Cake 147

Nougat Blanc 140

Rhubarb Friands with Crème Patisserie 134

Rocky Road 143

Rugelach with Apricot, Walnuts and Chocolate 137

Sandra's Melt-In-Your-Mouth Fudge 141

Banana, Pear and Date Tart 97

Barbecued Flatbreads with Sun-dried Tomato Pesto 19

Barbecued Fresh Figs with Creamy Blue Cheese 53

Barbecued Marinated Frenched Lamb Cutlets with Cucumber and Mint Relish 15

Basil Pesto 150

Basil's Ginger Beer Battered Fish with Cashew Dipping Sauce 26

Beans, Warm Haricot with Pine Nuts 64

Beef

Braised Beef Short Ribs 62

Classic Hamburgers 40

Roast Fillet of Beef, Herbed Eggplant and Salsa Verde 93

Standing Rib Roast of Beef with Caperberry Vinaigrette 114

Beetroot and Horseradish Condiment 165

Beetroot Jus 161

Beverages

Lavender Lemonade 22

Mint Tea 133

Biscuits, Chocolate Hazelnut 138

Blackcurrants with Baked Gala Apples 78

Braised Beef Short Ribs 62

Breakfast Salad 34

Bulgur Wheat, Zucchini and Corn Salad 46

Buttered Herbed Potatoes 123

C

Caesar Salad Dressing 155

Cake, Ginger and Cashew Celebration, with Glacé Fruit 128

Cake, Mango, Orange and Passionfruit 147

Caperberry Vinaigrette 153

Caramelised Onions 162

Caramelised Walnut and Apple Tart 75

Caramelised Walnuts (to make) 76

Carrot Soup with Scallops and Herb Leaves 83

Cashew Dipping Sauce 166

Celebrations Chapter

Buttered Herbed Potatoes 123

Celebration Seafood Salad 109

Christmas Crackers with Sweet Cherry Compote 124

Crayfish and Avocado Salad with David's Tangy Lemon Dressing 106

Double Lamb Forequarter with Roasted Vegetable Stuffing and Beetroot Jus 119

Ginger and Cashew Celebration Cake with Glacé Fruit 128

Parsnip and Shallots with Macadamia Nuts 116

Roasted Garlic Yorkshire Puddings 115

Standing Rib Roast of Beef with Caperberry Vinaigrette 114

Summer Pudding 127

Whole Roast Turkey with Old-fashioned Herb Stuffing, Trivet Potatoes and Pan Gravy 110

Celebration Seafood Salad 109

Cheesecake, Baked Chocolate and Amaretto 52

Cheese Toasties 132

Cherry Compote, Sweet 170

Chicken

Chicken Tulips in Red- and Blackcurrant Marinade 16

Corn-fed Chicken and Herbed Lentil Salad 36

Corn-fed Chicken with Vegetables and Tarragon Sauce 88

Mélange of Asparagus, Green Beans and Celery with Parsley Oil 121

Pork and Chicken Terrine with Dried Figs in Red Wine 59

Sage Chicken with Prosciutto and Vegetables 71

Chilli Saffron Vinaigrette 156

Chilli-spiced Almonds with Cumin 21

Chips, Homemade 43

Chocolate and Amaretto Cheesecake, Baked 52

Chocolate, Fudgy, and Ginger Mousse 99

Chocolate Hazelnut Biscuits 138

Chocolate (how to melt) 143

Chocolate Mice 144

Chorizo and Potato Salad 37

Christmas Crackers with Sweet Cherry Compote 124

Citrus Crème Fraîche 161

Clarified Butter (how to make) 134

Classic Hamburgers 40

Coffee Chapter

Cheese Toasties 132

Chocolate Hazelnut Biscuits 138

Chocolate Mice 144

Mango, Orange and Passionfruit Cake 147

Mint Tea 133

Nougat Blanc 140

Rhubarb Friands with Crème Patisserie 134

Rocky Road 143

Rugelach with Apricot, Walnuts and Chocolate 137

Sandra's Melt-In-Your-Mouth Fudge 141

Compote, Sweet Cherry 170

Condiments Chapter

Amaretto Dressing 169

Basil Pesto 150

Beetroot and Horseradish Condiment 165

Beetroot Jus 161

Caesar Salad Dressing 155

Caperberry Vinaigrette 153

Caramelised Onions 162

Cashew Dipping Sauce 166

Chilli Saffron Vinaigrette 156

Citrus Crème Fraîche 161

Cucumber and Mint Relish 165

David's Tangy Lemon Dressing 156

Dried Figs in Red Wine 171

Herbed Caper Sauce 155

Lemon Infused Olive Oil 168

Lime Wasabi Dressing 159

Mustard Mayonnaise 152

Parsley Infused Olive Oil 168

Passionfruit Syrup 169

Quince Jelly Dressing 159

Raspberry Vinaigrette 158

Roasted Garlic 162

Salsa Verde 153

Sandwich Mayonnaise 152

Spring Herb Dressing 166

Sweet Cherry Compote 170

Sun-dried Tomato Pesto 150

Yoghurt, Feta and Dill Dressing 158

Zucchini Pickle 163

Corn-fed Chicken and Herbed Lentil Salad 36

Corn-fed Chicken with Vegetables and Tarragon Sauce 88

Corn, Zucchini and Bulgur Wheat Salad 46

Crayfish and Avocado Salad with David's Tangy Lemon Dressing 106

Crayfish tails (how to cook and prepare) 106

Creamy Mushrooms with Port 60

Crème Brûlée, Golden Kiwifruit 94

Crème Fraîche, Citrus 161

Crème Patisserie (how to make) 135

Crepes, Saffron with Roasted Pumpkin and Cumin 28

Crostini (how to make) 109

Cucumber and Mint Relish 165

Cucumber and Radish Salad 84

D

Date, Pear and Banana Tart 97

Dave's Prosciutto Rolls 11

David's Tangy Lemon Dressing 156

Desserts

Baked Chocolate and Amaretto Cheesecake 52

Baked Gala Apples with Blackcurrants 78

Baked Pears in Verjuice with Vanilla 101

Barbecued Fresh Figs with Creamy Blue Cheese 53

Caramelised Walnut and Apple Tart 75

Chilli-spiced Almonds with Cumin 21

Christmas Crackers with Sweet Cherry Compote 124

Fudgy Chocolate and Ginger Mousse 99

Golden Kiwifruit Crème Brûlée 94

Kiwifruit, Passionfruit and Mint Salad with Amaretto Dressing 77

Lemon Frippery 55

Manuka Honey Ice Cream with Chilli-spiced Almonds with Cumin 102

Pear, Banana and Date Tart 97

Raspberries with Crème de Cassis 50

Rum Raisins 50

Strawberry and Rhubarb Shortcake 48

Summer Pudding 127

Whole Poached Plums 55

Dip, Mediterranean Feta and Herb 29

Dipping Sauce, Cashew 26

Double Lamb Forequarter with Roasted Vegetable Stuffing and Beetroot Jus 119

Dressings

Amaretto 169

Caesar Salad 155

Caperberry Vinaigrette 153

Chilli Saffron Vinaigrette 156

David's Tangy Lemon 156

Herbed Caper Sauce 155

Lime Wasabi 159

Mustard Mayonnaise 152

Quince Jelly 159

Raspberry Vinaigrette 158

Sandwich Mayonnaise 152

Spring Herb 166

Yoghurt, Feta and Dill 25

Dried Figs in Red Wine 171

Drinks chapter

Barbecued Flatbreads with Sun-dried Tomato Pesto 19

Barbecued Marinated Frenched Lamb Cutlets with Cucumber and Mint Relish 15

Basil's Ginger Beer Battered Fish with Cashew Dipping Sauce 26

Chicken Tulips in Red- and Blackcurrant Marinade 16

Chilli-spiced Almonds with Cumin 21

Dave's Prosciutto Rolls 11

Falafel with Yoghurt, Feta and Dill Dressing 25

Herbed Scampi Tails with Citrus Crème Fraîche 31

Lavender Lemonade 22

Mediterranean Feta and Herb Dip 29

Ricotta and Pesto Torte 12

Saffron Crepes with Roasted Pumpkin and Cumin 28

Warm Olives with Winter Herbs 20

E

Eggplant, Herbed, with Roast Fillet of Beef and Salsa Verde 93

F

Falafel with Yoghurt, Feta and Dill Dressing 25

Feta and Pumpkin Salad, Warm 45

Figs, Barbecued Fresh with Creamy Blue Cheese 53

Figs, Dried, in Red Wine 171

Fish

Basil's Ginger Beer Battered Fish with Cashew Dipping Sauce 26

Salmon Wrapped in Nori with Lime Wasabi Dressing 84

West Coast Whitebait with Zucchini Ribbons 86

Flatbreads, Barbecued, with Sun-dried Tomato Pesto 19

Frenched Lamb Racks with Lemon and Peppercorn Paste and Spring Herb Dressing 90

Friands, Rhubarb with Crème Patisserie 134

Frippery, Lemon 55

Fudge, Sandra's Melt-In-Your-Mouth 141

Fudgy Chocolate and Ginger Mousse 99

G

Galette, Leek, Thyme and Feta 66

Garlic, Roasted 162

Ginger and Cashew Celebration Cake with Glacé Fruit 128

Ginger and Fudgy Chocolate Mousse 99

Golden Kiwifruit Crème Brûlée 94

Gravy, Pan 111

H

Haricot Beans, Warm, with Pine Nuts 64

Hamburgers, Classic 40

Herbed Caper Sauce 155

Herbed Eggplant 93

Herbed Lentil Salad 36

174

Herbed Scampi Tails with Citrus Crème Fraîche 31

Homemade Chips 43

Honeyed Kumara Mash 64

I

Ice Cream, Manuka Honey, with Chilli-spiced Almonds with Cumin 102

J

Jus, Beetroot 161

K

Kiwifruit, Golden, Crème Brûlée 94

Kiwifruit, Passionfruit and Mint Salad with Amaretto Dressing 77

Kumara Mash, Honeyed 64

L

Lamb

    Barbecued Marinated Frenched Lamb Cutlets with Cucumber and Mint Relish 15

    Double Lamb Forequarter with Roasted Vegetable Stuffing and Beetroot Jus 119

    Frenched Lamb Racks with Lemon and Peppercorn Paste and Spring Herb Dressing 90

Lavender Lemonade 22

Leek, Thyme and Feta Galette 66

Lemonade, Lavender 22

Lemon and Peppercorn Paste 90

Lemon Frippery 55

Lemon Infused Olive Oil 168

Lentil Salad, Herbed 36

Lime Wasabi Dressing 159

M

Macadamia Nuts with Parsnip and Shallots 116

Mango, Orange and Passionfruit Cake 147

Manuka Honey Ice Cream with Chilli-spiced Almonds with Cumin 102

Marinade, Apple Syrup 68

Marinade, Red- and Blackcurrant 16

Marshmallow (how to make) 143

Mayonnaise, Mustard 152

Mayonnaise, Sandwich 152

Mediterranean Feta and Herb Dip 29

Mélange of Asparagus, Green Beans and Celery with Parsley Oil 121

Mint Tea 133

Mousse, Fudgy Chocolate and Ginger 99

Mushrooms, Creamy, with Port 60

Mustard Mayonnaise 152

N

Nougat Blanc 140

O

Old-fashioned Herb Stuffing 110

Olive Oil, Lemon Infused 168

Olive Oil, Parsley Infused 168

Olives, Warm, with Winter Herbs 20

Onions, Caramelised 162

Orange, Mango and Passionfruit Cake 147

P

Pan Gravy 110

Parsley Infused Olive Oil 168

Parsnip and Shallots with Macadamia Nuts 116

Passionfruit, Kiwifruit and Mint Salad with Amaretto Dressing 77

Passionfruit, Mango and Orange Cake 147

Passionfruit Syrup 169

Paste, Lemon and Peppercorn 90

Pastry (how to make)

    Sweet Pastry 97

    Sweet Short Pastry 75

    Yeast Dough Pastry 67

Pear, Banana and Date Tart 97

Pears, Baked, in Verjuice with Vanilla 101

Pesto and Ricotta Torte 12

Pesto, Basil 150

Pesto, Sun-dried Tomato 150

Pickle, Zucchini 163

Pine Nuts with Warm Haricot Beans 64

Plums, Whole Poached 55

Pork and Chicken Terrine with Dried Figs in Red Wine 59

Pork Belly in Apple Syrup Marinade 68

Posh Chapter

    Baked Pears in Verjuice with Vanilla 101

    Carrot Soup with Scallops and Herb Leaves 83

    Corn-fed Chicken with Vegetables and Tarragon Sauce 88

    Frenched Lamb Racks with Lemon and Peppercorn Paste and Spring Herb Dressing 90

    Fudgy Chocolate and Ginger Mousse 99

    Golden Kiwifruit Crème Brûlée 94

    Manuka Honey Ice Cream with Chilli-spiced Almonds with Cumin 102

    Pear, Banana and Date Tart 97

    Roast Fillet of Beef, Herbed Eggplant and Salsa Verde 93

    Salmon Wrapped in Nori with Lime Wasabi Dressing 84

    West Coast Whitebait with Zucchini Ribbons 86

Potato and Chorizo Salad 37

Potatoes, Buttered Herbed 123

Prosciutto Rolls, Dave's 11

Prosciutto with Sage Chicken and Vegetables 71

Pudding, Summer 127

Purslane and Spinach Salad with Quince Jelly Dressing 65

Q

Quince Jelly Dressing 159

R

Raisins, Rum 50

Raspberries with Crème de Cassis 50

Raspberry Vinaigrette 158

Red- and Blackcurrant Marinade 16

Relish, Cucumber and Mint 165

Rhubarb and Strawberry Shortcake 48

Rhubarb Friands with Crème Patisserie 134

Ricotta and Pesto Torte 12

Roasted Garlic 162

Roasted Garlic Yorkshire Puddings 115

Roasted Vegetable Stuffing 120

Roasted Winter Vegetable Tarte Tartin 72

Roast Fillet of Beef, Herbed Eggplant and Salsa Verde 93

Rocky Road 143

Rugelach with Apricot, Walnuts and Chocolate 137

Rum Raisins 50

S

Saffron Crepes with Roasted Pumpkin and Cumin 28

Sage Chicken with Prosciutto and Vegetables 71

Salads

    Breakfast 34

    Celebration Seafood Salad 109

    Corn-fed Chicken and Herbed Lentil 36

    Crayfish and Avocado Salad with David's Tangy Lemon Dressing 106

    Cucumber and Radish Salad 84

    Potato and Chorizo 37

Spinach and Purslane Salad with Quince Jelly Dressing 65

Warm Pumpkin and Feta 45

Zucchini, Corn and Bulgur Wheat 46

Salmon Wrapped in Nori with Lime Wasabi Dressing 84

Salsa Verde 153

Sandra's Melt-In-Your-Mouth Fudge 141

Sandwich Mayonnaise 152

Sauce, Herbed Caper 155

Sauce, Tarragon 89

Scallops with Carrot Soup and Herb Leaves 83

Scampi Tails, Herbed, with Citrus Crème Fraîche 31

Seafood

Carrot Soup with Scallops and Herb Leaves 83

Celebration Seafood Salad 109

Crayfish and Avocado Salad with David's Tangy Lemon Dressing 106

Herbed Scampi Tails with Citrus Crème Fraîche 31

Shortcake, Strawberry and Rhubarb 48

Soup, Carrot with Scallops and Herb Leaves 83

Spinach and Purslane Salad with Quince Jelly Dressing 65

Spring Herb Dressing 166

Standing Rib Roast of Beef with Caperberry Vinaigrette 114

Strawberry and Rhubarb Shortcake 48

Stuffing, Old-fashioned Herb 110

Stuffing, Roasted Vegetable 120

Summer Chapter

Baked Chocolate and Amaretto Cheesecake 52

Barbecued Fresh Figs with Creamy Blue Cheese 53

Breakfast Salad 34

Classic Hamburgers 40

Corn-fed Chicken and Herbed Lentil Salad 36

Homemade Chips 43

Lemon Frippery 55

Potato and Chorizo Salad 37

Raspberries with Crème de Cassis 50

Rum Raisins 50

Strawberry and Rhubarb Shortcake 48

Warm Pumpkin and Feta Salad 45

Whole Poached Plums 55

Zucchini, Corn and Bulgur Wheat Salad 46

Summer Pudding 127

Sun-dried Tomato Pesto 150

Sweet Cherry Compote 170

Syrup, Passionfruit 169

T

Tarragon Sauce 89

Tart, Caramelised Walnut and Apple 75

Tarte Tartin, Roasted Winter Vegetable 72

Tart, Pear, Banana and Date 97

Tea, Mint 132

Terrine, Pork and Chicken, with Dried Figs in Red Wine 59

Toasties, Cheese 132

Torte, Ricotta and Pesto 12

Turkey, Whole Roast with Old-fashioned Herb Stuffing, Trivet Potatoes and Pan Gravy 110

V

Vegetable accompaniments

Buttered Herbed Potatoes 123

Corn, Zucchini and Bulgur Wheat Salad 46

Homemade Chips 43

Honeyed Kumara Mash 64

Mélange of Asparagus, Green Beans and Celery with Parsley Oil 121

Parsnip and Shallots with Macadamia Nuts 116

Potato and Chorizo Salad 37

Roasted Winter Vegetable Tarte Tartin 72

Warm Haricot Beans with Pine Nuts 64

Warm Pumpkin and Feta Salad 45

Vinaigrette, Caperberry 153

Vinaigrette, Chilli Saffron 156

Vinaigrette, Raspberry 158

W

Walnut, Caramelised and Apple Tart 75

Warm Haricot Beans with Pine Nuts 64

Warm Olives with Winter Herbs 20

Warm Pumpkin and Feta Salad 45

West Coast Whitebait with Zucchini Ribbons 86

Whole Poached Plums 55

Whole Roast Turkey with Old-fashioned Herb Stuffing, Trivet Potatoes and Pan Gravy 110

Winter Chapter

Baked Gala Apples with Blackcurrants 78

Braised Beef Short Ribs 62

Caramelised Walnut and Apple Tart 75

Creamy Mushrooms with Port 60

Honeyed Kumara Mash 64

Kiwifruit, Passionfruit and Mint Salad with Amaretto Dressing 77

Leek, Thyme and Feta Galette 66

Pork and Chicken Terrine with Dried Figs in Red Wine 59

Pork Belly in Apple Syrup Marinade 68

Roasted Winter Vegetable Tarte Tartin 72

Sage Chicken with Prosciutto and Vegetables 71

Spinach and Purslane Salad with Quince Jelly Dressing 65

Warm Haricot Beans with Pine Nuts 64

Y

Yoghurt, Feta and Dill Dressing 158

Yorkshire Puddings, Roasted Garlic 115

Z

Zucchini, Corn and Bulgur Wheat Salad 46

Zucchini Pickle 163